First Lines
Poems written in youth, from Herbert to Heaney

First Lines

*poems
written in youth,
from Herbert to
Heaney*

edited and introduced by
Jon Stallworthy

CARCANET

First published in Great Britain 1987 by
Carcanet Press Limited
208-212 Corn Exchange Buildings
Manchester M4 3BQ

Carcanet
198 Sixth Avenue
New York, New York 10013

British Library Cataloguing in Publication Data

First Lines : poems written in youth from
  Herbert to Heaney.
  1. English poetry
  I. Stallworthy, Jon
  821'.008   PR1175

ISBN 0-85635-476-7

The publishers acknowledge the financial assistance
of the Arts Council of Great Britain

Typeset in 10pt Palatino by Bryan Williamson, Manchester
Printed in England by SRP Ltd, Exeter

Contents

Introduction

Poets and readers of poetry are often asked, and often unable to answer, "When did Keats – or why did Yeats, or how does one – begin to write poems?"

This anthology has been compiled in the belief that these are important questions; important in themselves and important to the next generation of poets and readers of poetry. Like most important questions, they are at best difficult, and at worst impossible to answer. Only the poets know when or why or how they began to write poems, and as they grow older, they are inclined to forget or to "remember" that they wrote poems earlier, or better, or for other reasons than they did. Few of the poems in this collection will be the very first lines their poets ever wrote, and many will have been improved before being allowed to take their place in the *Collected Works*. Even so, viewed together, these poems of childhood and adolescence by fifty-eight hands that were later to write many of the finest poems in the English language do reveal some interesting common characteristics.

Many show a knowledge – by today's standards, a remarkable knowledge – of other poetry. Pope at twelve takes his theme from Horace's *Epode II*, Wordsworth at sixteen borrows from Milton, Keats at eighteen proclaims a debt to Spenser, Hardy at seventeen is under the influence of Wordsworth, Heaney at nineteen under that of Hopkins. *Influence* – far from showing a lack of originality, as reviewers of first books sometimes suggest – is revealed as a vital stage in a poet's development. Just as young painters and sculptors through history have worked in the studios of older, established artists before following the call of their own imagination, it is hard to think of a major poet who has not been well and widely read in the poetry of earlier times – even if little trace of this appears in his or her best-known work.

There are indications that the earliest literary influence on many poets may be nursery rhymes. "There was an old woman who lived in a shoe" would seem to underlie Byron's "In Nottingham county there lives at Swan Green, / As curst an old lady as ever was seen;" Shelley's verses on a cat owe at least their rhyme scheme to "Little Miss Muffet"; and "Mary had a little lamb" never underwent a stranger mutation than in Christina Rossetti's infant imagination: "Cecilia never went to school / Without her gladiator." Children like rhyme, often supposing it the principal ingredient of poetry, and it is present in the juvenilia of all but three of the poets represented here; Swinburne and Hardy, who write in blank verse (but became inveterate rhymers), and William Carlos Williams.

Nursery rhymes also introduce children to metre, and Williams is the only one of these fifty-eight poets whose ear is not attuned to formal metrics; though it should be added that his lines have an assured and strongly individual cadence:

> A black, black cloud
> flew over the sun
> driven by fierce flying
> rain.

The three stresses in each of the first three lines give them a delicate unity, and set up expectations that are brilliantly upset by the final – deferred and all-important – monosyllable.

Predictably, the majority of these poems are iambic, but Byron, Clare, Beddoes, and Dylan Thomas all make good use of anapaests. Most interesting, however, are the poems of those who have learnt to mix their metres: notably Poe's "To Helen", Emily Brontë's "A.G.A. to A.E.", and Wilde's "Requiescat".

A good index of the level of technical sophistication reached by these (or, indeed, any) poets is the manner in which they bring their poems to a close. Frequently this will involve a return that brings the reader full circle. Wordsworth, addressing his "Dear native regions", foretells that "whenso'er my course shall end", the eye of memory will be fixed on them. This prophecy his poem, in advance, fulfils. As its "course" approaches its end, the sixteen-year-old poet draws – subconsciously, no doubt – on the last section of "Lycidas" for his image of the sunset, whose light brings the sun/son (Milton had used the same pun) back to "the dear hills where first he rose".

Clough's "Thoughts of Home" carry him over "many a wave" to America, where he had "longed for ... England's breezes", before returning him via the contemplation of "a worse and wider sea" to the window with its view of children at play that first prompted his poem. Joyce's painterly "Dublin Interior" has a similar circular trajectory, as has Sidney Keyes' "Elegy" for his grandfather. This – with the exception of Poe's "To Helen", perhaps the best poem in the book – begins:

> April again, and it is a year again
> Since you walked out and slammed the door
> Leaving us tangled in your words.

Subsequent stanzas being "It is a year again" and "A year again", the repetition mirroring the repetition of the months and years, and preparing for the final lines: "We shall never forget nor escape you, nor make terms / With your enemies, the swift departing years." So unobtrusive is this structure, so personal the cadence, of this minor masterpiece, that I find it even more moving than Poe's superbly classical address "To Helen".

In an architectural sense more ambitious, if less successful overall, are certain of the longer poems included here. Strictly speaking, one cannot claim originality for Cowley's re-telling of the tale of Pyramus and Thisbe (taken no doubt from *A Midsummer Night's Dream*, as the closing "Epitaph" takes its inspiration from Shakespeare's poem, "The Phoenix and the Turtle"), or for Frost's re-telling of W.H. Prescott's account of the Spanish Conquistadores' retreat from Tenochtitlan; but these poems, and Benét's "The Hemp", are nonetheless remarkable achievements for poets aged ten, sixteen, and seventeen respectively.

It is interesting, but should not be surprising, how "traditional" appear the early poems of those later regarded as revolutionary: Blake, Pound, Eliot, and Cummings, for example. All learnt their craft in other men's studios before they judged it was time to leave and go their own way. It cannot be accident that these, like D.H. Lawrence and Robert Lowell (neither represented here), all made themselves masters of rhyme and metre before turning to the free verse they found better suited to their own particular voices. Most poets would agree that free verse is easier to write badly, but harder to write well, than formal verse. The poet with no regular rhyme scheme, no fixed number of metrical feet to give shape to his poem, has only his ear to guide him. If his ear is not so trained that it can distinguish between a good and bad sequence of vowel sounds, for example, or between a good and a bad line-ending, the poem is likely to collapse into pretentious prose.

"An immature poet", wrote W.H. Auden in an essay on the poetry of D.H. Lawrence, "if he has a real talent, usually begins to exhibit quite early a distinctive style of his own; however obvious the influence of some older writer may be, there is something original in his manner or, at least, great technical competence." He goes on to say that, in Lawrence's case, this was not so; "it took him a long time to find the appropriate style for him to speak in".

The poems collected here prove the truth of Auden's statement. Most show a considerable degree of technical competence, and

11

in many of them a reader familiar with that poet's later work can hear the same voice speaking; the voice that distinguishes one poet – as it distinguishes one person – from another. The extract from Wordsworth's poem "Composed in Anticipation of leaving school", though its tetrameters move more briskly than the pentameters of *The Prelude*, carries the same clear "voice print". Similarly, both the intonation and the fluent grace of "Memory" would proclaim it to be from the same hand and voice as Tennyson's "The Brook", even if its subject and perspective did not make that apparent. The authorship of Dickinson's "A Valentine" is harder to establish, until one perceives that every line divides at a central caesura. Re-align a couple as

> The *worm* doth woo the *mortal*,
> death claims a living bride,
> Night unto day is married,
> morn unto eventide...

and one hears the triple-stressed cadence of:

> I felt a Funeral in my Brain,
> And Mourners to and fro
> Kept treading – treading – till it seemed
> That Sense was breaking through –

Douglas's coolly clinical voice is as unmistakable in ".303" as in "How to Kill"; but perhaps the most striking example of this phenomenon is offered by "Wild West", a poem written by the fifteen-year-old Ted Hughes and first printed in the Mexborough Secondary School magazine. Unfortunately it has proved impossible to reproduce it here: a brief quotation, however, will make my point. In the course of a "shoot-out" in "Wild West",

> Carson McReared the Terrible sent
> A leaden slug weighing 200 grains
> Slap into Kincaid's squirming brains.

Who could doubt that those "squirming brains" came from any imagination, voice, hand but those that would later render a thrush with a worm as "Nothing but bounce and stab / And a ravening second"?

If one can seldom answer satisfactorily the question "*When* did Keats, or Christina Rossetti, begin to write poems?" the *why* and the *how* of it are easier. Poets usually begin to write poems because they have read other people's and like them so much they want to write one themselves. Some of the best have not been deterred by having nothing particularly important to say. There are times when we all simply want to hear the sound of our own voices to reassure ourselves that we exist.

Few English-speaking poets seem to have found their voices as early as certain composers "found out musical tunes": Mozart's first pieces were written at four and Liszt's operetta *Don Sancho* was performed when he was fourteen. Music is, of course, the more social art, and the child of musical parents is likely to be introduced to instruments and scores before the child of literary parents is introduced to the technicalities of poetry. Even so, it is surprising how few notable poets have poets for parents, or children. This should be a source of encouragement to all those who like poems and want to write them, but have no literary background. Christopher Smart may have written a poem at four, but it seems likely that Edward Thomas wrote his first at thirty-six.

*

Several friends have helped in the preparation of this anthology and I should particularly like to thank the following: Mr Hugo Brunner, Dr Jacqueline Doyle, Mr John Murray, C.B.E., Mrs Karina Williamson, Mr Anthony Thwaite, and my publishers, Dr Robyn Marsack and Mr Michael Schmidt.

George Herbert
1593-1633

In December 1609, Herbert sent two sonnets to his mother as a New Year's gift from Cambridge. He wrote in the accompanying letter: 'But I fear the heat of my late ague hath dried up those springs, by which scholars say, the Muses used to take up their habitations. However, I need not their help, to reprove the vanity of those many love-poems, that are daily writ and consecrated to Venus: nor to bewail that so few are writ, that look toward God and Heaven. For my own part, my meaning (dear Mother) is in these sonnets, to declare my resolution to be, that my poor abilities in poetry, shall be all, and ever consecrated to God's glory.'

[SONNETS

SENT TO HIS MOTHER AS A NEW YEAR'S GIFT FROM CAMBRIDGE]

My God, where is that ancient heat towards Thee
  Wherewith whole shoals of martyrs once did burn,
Beside their other flames? Doth Poetry
  Wear Venus' livery? only serve her turn?
Why are not sonnets made of Thee, and lays
  Upon Thine altar burnt? Cannot Thy love
Heighten a spirit to sound out Thy praise
  As well as any she? Cannot Thy Dove
Outstrip their Cupid easily in flight?
  Or, since Thy ways are deep, and still the same,
  Will not a verse run smooth that bears Thy Name?
Why doth that fire, which by Thy power and might
  Each breast does feel, no braver fuel choose
  Then that which one day worms may chance refuse?

Sure, Lord, there is enough in Thee to dry
  Oceans of ink; for, as the Deluge did
Cover the earth, so doth Thy Majesty.
  Each cloud distills Thy praise, and doth forbid
Poets to turn it to another use;
  Roses and lilies speak Thee, and to make
A pair of cheeks of them, is Thy abuse.
  Why should I women's eyes for crystal take?
Such poor invention burns in their low mind,

Whose fire is wild, and doth not upward go
  To praise, and on Thee, Lord, some ink bestow.
Open the bones, and you shall nothing find
  In the best face but filth; when, Lord, in Thee
  The beauty lies in the discovery.

Aged 16

John Milton
1608-1674

John Aubrey, in his *Brief Lives*, says that Milton was a poet at the age of ten and reports his brother, Christopher Milton, as saying that, 'when he was very young, he studied very hard, and sat up very late, commonly till twelve or one a clock at night, and his father ordered the maid to sit up for him, and in those years (10) composed many copies of verses which might well become a riper age'. The earliest surviving examples of his work were written in 1624, his last year at St Paul's School.

In this poem, he versifies the psalmist's retelling of the Bible's account of how God rescued Moses and the Israelites from captivity in Egypt; killing the eldest sons of their oppressors; parting the waters of the Red Sea so that they could cross in safety; drowning the Pharaoh's soldiers that pursued them; helping them defeat their other enemies; and leading them at last to their 'Promised Land'.

PSALM 136

Let us with a gladsome mind
Praise the Lord, for he is kind,
   For his mercies aye endure,
   Ever faithful, ever sure.

Let us blaze his name abroad,
For of gods he is the God;
   For, etc.

O let us his praises tell,
That doth the wrathful tyrants quell.
   For, etc.

That with his miracles doth make
Amazéd heaven and earth to shake.
   For, etc.

That by his wisdom did create
The painted heavens so full of state.
   For, etc.

That did the solid Earth ordain
To rise above the watery plain.
   For, etc.

That by his all-commanding might,
Did fill the new-made world with light.
   For, etc.

And caused the golden-tressèd sun,
All the day long his course to run.
   For, etc.

The hornèd moon to shine by night,
Amongst her spangled sisters bright.
   For, etc.

He with his thunder-clasping hand,
Smote the first-born of Egypt land.
   For, etc.

And in despite of Pharaoh fell,
He brought from thence his Israel.
   For, etc.

The ruddy waves he cleft in twain,
Of the Erythrean main.
   For, etc.

The floods stood still like walls of glass,
While the Hebrew bands did pass.
   For, etc.

But full soon they did devour
The tawny king with all his power.
   For, etc.

His chosen people he did bless
In the wasteful wilderness.
   For, etc.

In bloody battle he brought down
Kings of prowess and renown.
   For, etc.

He foiled bold Seon and his host,
That ruled the Amorrean coast.
   For, etc.

And large-limbed Og he did subdue,
With all his over-hardy crew.
    For, etc.

And to his servant Israel,
He gave their land therein to dwell.
    For, etc.

He hath with a piteous eye
Beheld us in our misery.
    For, etc.

And freed us from the slavery
Of the invading enemy.
    For, etc.

All living creatures he doth feed,
And with full hand supplies their need.
    For, etc.

Let us therefore warble forth
His mighty majesty and worth.
    For, etc.

That his mansion hath on high
Above the reach of mortal eye.
    For his mercies aye endure,
    Ever faithful, ever sure.

Aged 15

Abraham Cowley
1618-1667

Three years before he left Westminster School, Cowley published his first volume of verse, *Poetical Blossoms*. The fifteen-year-old poet was popularly believed to be only thirteen at the time. A number of poems in the book had been written yet earlier: in a prefatory epistle to the second edition, Cowley admitted that 'Pyramus and Thisbe' had been composed when he was only ten:

> Reader! (I know not yet whether gentle or no) some I know have been angry (I dare not assume the honour of their envy) at my poetical boldness, and blamed in mine what commends other fruits, earliness. ...It is not, I am sure, the first book which has lighted tobacco, or been employed by cooks and grocers. If in all men's judgments it suffer shipwreck it shall something content me that it hath pleased myself and the bookseller. In it you shall find one argument (and I hope I shall need no more) to confute unbelievers, which is, that as mine age, and, consequently, experience (which is yet but little), have increased, so they have not left my poesy flagging behind them. I should not be angry to see any one burn my Pyramus and Thisbe; nay, I would do it myself, but that I hope a pardon may easily be gotten for the errors of ten years of age.

PYRAMUS AND THISBE

1

Where Babylon's high walls erected were
By mighty Ninus' wife, two houses joined.
One Thisbe lived in, Pyramus the fair
In the other; earth ne'er boasted such a pair.
The very senseless walls themselves combined,
And grew in one, just like their masters' mind.

2

Thisbe all other women did excel,
The Queen of Love less lovely was than she;
And Pyramus more sweet than tongue can tell,
Nature grew proud in framing them so well:
But Venus envying they so fair should be,
Bids her son Cupid show his cruelty.

3

The all-subduing god his bow did bend,
And doth prepare his most remorseless dart,

Which he unseen into their hearts did send,
And so was Love the cause of Beauty's end:
But could he see, he had not wrought their smart;
For pity, sure, would have o'ercome his heart.

4

Like as a bird which in the net is ta'en,
By struggling more entangles in the gin,
So they who in love's labyrinth remain,
With striving never can a freedom gain:
The way to enter's broad; but being in,
No art, no labour, can an exit win.

5

These lovers, though their parents did reprove
Their fires, and watched their deed with jealousy,
Though in these storms no comfort could remove
The various doubt and fears that cool hot love;
Though he not hers, nor she his face could see,
Yet this did not abolish Love's decree.

6

For age had cracked the wall which did them part;
This the inanimate couple soon did spy,
And here their inward sorrows did impart,
Unlading the sad burden of their heart.
Though Love be blind, this shows he can descry
A way to lessen his own misery.

7

Oft to the friendly cranny they resort,
And feed themselves with the celestial air
Of odoriferous breath; no other sport
They could enjoy, yet think the time but short,
And with that it again renewéd were,
To suck each other's breath for ever there.

8

Sometimes they did exclaim against their fate,
And sometimes they accused imperial Jove;
Sometimes repent their flames; but all too late;
The arrow could not be recalled; their state
Ordained was first by Jupiter above,
And Cupid had appointed they should love.

They cursed the wall that did their kisses part,
And to the stones their dolorous words they sent,
As if they saw the sorrow of their heart,
And by their tears could understand their smart;
But it was hard, and knew not what they meant,
Nor with their sighs, alas! would it relent.

This in effect they said: 'Curs'd Wall! O why
Wilt thou our bodies sever, whose true love
Breaks through all thy flinty cruelty;
For both our souls so closely joinéd lie,
That nought but angry Death can them remove,
And though he part them, yet they'll meet above.'

Abortive tears from their fair eyes straight flowed,
And dimmed the lovely splendour of their sight,
Which seemed like Titan, whilst some watery cloud
O'erspreads his face, and his bright beams doth shroud;
Till Vesper chased away the conquered light,
And forceth them, though loth, to bid good-night.

But ere Aurora, usher to the day,
Began with welcome lustre to appear,
The lovers rise, and at that cranny they
Thus to each other their thoughts open lay,
With many a sigh, many a speaking tear,
Whose grief the pitying Morning blushed to hear.

'Dear love!' said Pyramus, 'how long shall we,
Like fairest flowers, not gathered in their prime,
Waste precious youth, and let advantage flee,
Till we bewail, at last, our cruelty
Upon ourselves? for beauty, though it shine
Like day, will quickly find an evening-time.

'Therefore, sweet Thisbe! let us meet this night
At Ninus' tomb, without the city wall,

Under the mulberry-tree, with berries white
Abounding, there to enjoy our wished delight:
For mounting love stopped in its course doth fall,
And longed-for, yet untasted, joy, kills all.

15

'What though our cruel parents angry be!
What though our friends, alas! are, too, unkind!
Time, now propitious, may anon deny,
And soon hold back fit opportunity.
Who lets slip Fortune, her shall never find;
Occasion once passed by is bald behind.'

16

She soon agreed to that which he required,
For little wooing needs where both consent;
What he so long had pleaded she desired;
Which Venus seeing, with blind Chance conspired,
And many a charming accent to her sent,
That she, at last, would frustrate their intent.

17

Thus beauty is by Beauty's means undone,
Striving to close those eyes that make her bright;
Just like the moon, which seeks to eclipse the sun,
Whence all her splendour, all her beams, do come:
So she who fetcheth lustre from their sight,
Doth purpose to destroy their glorious light.

18

Unto the mulberry-tree sweet Thisbe came,
Where having rested long, at last she 'gan
Against her Pyramus for to exclaim,
Whilst various thoughts turmoil her troubled brain,
And imitating thus the silver swan,
A little while before her death, she sang.

SONG

'Come, Love! why stayest thou? the night
Will vanish ere we taste delight:
The moon obscures herself from sight,
Thou absent, whose eyes give her light.

23

'Come quickly, Dear! be brief as Time,
Or we by Morn shall be o'erta'en,
Love's joy's thine own as well as mine;
Spend not, therefore, time in vain.'

19

Here doubtful thoughts broke off her pleasant song,
Against her love for staying she 'gan cry;
Her Pyramus she thought did tarry long,
That his absence did her too much wrong;
Then, betwixt longing hope and jealousy
She fears, yet 's loth to tax his loyalty.

20

Sometimes she thinks that he hath her forsaken;
Sometimes that danger hath befallen him;
She fears that he another love hath taken;
Which being but imagined soon doth waken
Numberless thoughts, which on her heart do fling
Fears, that her future fate too truly sing.

21

While she thus musing sat, ran from the wood
An angry lion to the crystal springs
Near to that place, who coming from his food,
His chaps were all besmeared with crimson blood:
Swifter than thought sweet Thisbe straight begins
To fly from him; fear gave her swallows' wings.

22

As she avoids the lion, her desire
Bids her to stay, lest Pyramus should come
And be devoured by the stern lion's ire,
So she for ever burn in unquenched fire;
But fear expels all reasons; she doth run
Into a darksome cave ne'er seen by sun.

23

With haste she let her looser mantle fall;
Which when the enragéd lion did espy,
With bloody teeth he tore 't in pieces small.
Whilst Thisbe ran and looked not back at all:
For could the senseless beast her face descry,
It had not done her such an injury.

24

24

The night half wasted, Pyramus did come;
Who seeing printed in the subtle sand
The lion's paw, and by the fountain some
Of Thisbe's garment, sorrow struck him dumb;
Just like a marble statue did he stand,
Cut by some skilful graver's cunning hand.

25

Recovering breath, 'gainst Fate he 'gan to exclaim,
Washing with tears the torn and bloody weed:
'I may,' said he, 'myself for her death blame,
Therefore my blood shall wash away that shame;
Since she is dead, whose beauty doth exceed
All that frail man can either hear or read.'

26

This spoke, he his sharp sword drew, and said,
'Receive thou my red blood, as a due debt
Unto thy constant love, to which 'tis paid:
I straight will meet thee in the pleasant shade
Of cool Elysium, where we being met,
Shall taste the joys that here we could not get.'

27

Then through his breast thrusting his sword, life hies
From him, and he makes haste to seek his fair;
And as upon the crimsoned ground he lies,
His blood spurted up upon the mulberries,
With which the unspotted berries stainéd were,
And ever since with red they coloured are.

28

At last came Thisbe from the den, for fear
Of disappointing Pyramus, being she
Was bound by promise for to meet him there;
But when she saw the berries changéd were
From white to black, she knew not certainly
It was the place where they agreed to be.

29

With what delight, from the dark cave she came,
Thinking to tell how she escaped the beast;

But when she saw her Pyramus lie slain,
In what perplexity did she sad remain!
She tears her golden hair, and beats her breast,
All signs of raging sorrow she expressed.

30

She cries 'gainst mighty love, and then doth take
His bleeding body from the moistened ground;
She kisses his pale face, till she doth make
It red with kissing, and then seeks to wake
His parting soul with mournful words; and 's wound
Washes with tears, that her sweet speech confound.

31

But afterwards recovering breath, quoth she,
'Alas! what chance hath parted thee and I?
O tell what evil hath befallen to thee,
That of thy death I may a partner be;
Tell Thisbe what hath caused this tragedy.'
He, hearing Thisbe's name, lifts up his eye,

32

And on his love he raised his dying head,
Where striving long for breath, at last, said he,
'O Thisbe! I am hasting to the dead,
And cannot heal that wound my fear hath bred.
Farewell, sweet Thisbe! we must parted be,
For angry Death will force me go from thee.'

33

Life did from him, he from his mistress, part,
Leaving his love to languish here in woe.
What shall she do? how shall she ease her heart?
Or with what language speak her inward smart?
Usurping passion reason doth o'erflow;
She swears that with her Pyramus she'll go.

34

Then takes the sword wherewith her love was slain,
With Pyramus his crimson blood warm still,
And said, 'O stay, blessed soul! that so we twain
May go together where we shall remain
In endless joys and never fear the ill
Of grudging friends.' – Then she herself did kill.

To tell what grief their parents did sustain,
Were more than my rude quill can overcome;
Many a tear they spent, but all in vain;
For weeping calls not back the dead again.
They both were layéd in one grave, life done,
And these few words were writ upon the tomb.

EPITAPH

Underneath this marble stone
Lie two beauties joined in one:
Two whose loves death could not sever,
For both lived, both died together.

Two whose souls, being too divine
For earth, in their own sphere now shine:
Who have left their loves to fame,
And their earth to earth again.

Aged 10

Alexander Pope
1688-1744

Pope's poetical talents showed themselves early. In a letter to a friend accompanying a copy of his 'Ode on Solitude', he said it was 'written when I was not twelve years', but it seems almost certain that he revised it considerably before publishing it. Its classical echoes seem to derive from Abraham Cowley's translations of a group of Latin poems by Horace, Martial and Seneca.

ODE ON SOLITUDE

Happy the man, whose wish and care
A few paternal acres bound,
Content to breathe his native air,
                In his own ground.

Whose herds with milk, whose fields with bread,
Whose flocks supply him with attire,
Whose trees in summer yield him shade,
                In winter fire.

Blest! who can unconcern'dly find
Hours, days, and years slide soft away,
In health of body, peace of mind,
                Quiet by day,

Sound sleep by night; study and ease
Together mixed; sweet recreation,
And innocence, which most does please,
                With meditation.

Thus let me live, unseen, unknown;
Thus unlamented let me die;
Steal from the world, and not a stone
                Tell where I lie.

Aged 12?

Samuel Johnson
1709-1784

When James Boswell was at work on his *Life of Johnson*, Edmund Hector, a former schoolfellow, supplied a number of Johnson's early poems. 'On a Daffodil' is the earliest of these. 'The Daffodaill was wrote between his 15th and 16th Year,' Hector reported to Boswell, 'As it was not characteristick of the Flower He never much lik'd it.'

ON A DAFFODIL, THE FIRST FLOWER
THE AUTHOR HAD SEEN THAT YEAR

Hail! lovely flower, first honour of the year,
Hail! beauteous earnest of approaching Spring;
Whose early buds unusual glories wear,
And of a fruitful year fair omens bring.

Be thou the favourite of the indulgent sky,
Nor feel th' inclemencies of wintry air,
May no rude blasts thy sacred bloom destroy;
May storms howl gently o'er, and learn to spare.

May lambent zephyrs gently wave thy head,
And balmy spirits through thy foliage play,
May the morn's earliest tears on thee be shed
And thou impearled with dew, appear more gay.

May throngs of beauteous virgins 'round thee crowd,
And view thy charms with no malignant eyes;
Then scorn those flowers, to which the Egyptians bowed,
Which prostrate Memphis owned her deities.

If mixed with these, divine Cleora smile,
Cleora's smiles a genial warmth dispense,
New verdure every fading leaf shall fill,
And thou shalt flourish by her influence.

But while I sing, the nimble moments fly,
See! Sol's bright chariot seeks the western main,
And ah! behold the shrivelling blossoms die,
So late admired, and praised, alas! in vain.

With grief this emblem of mankind I see,
Like one awakened from a pleasing dream,
Cleora's self fair flower shall fade like thee;
Alike must fall the poet and his theme.

Aged 15

Thomas Gray
1716-1771

When Thomas Gray was at Eton, he and three of his friends formed the 'Quadruple Alliance': 'Celadon' (Horace Walpole), 'Orozmades' (Gray himself), 'Favonius' or 'Zephyrus' (Richard West), and 'Almanzor' (Thomas Ashton) – dedicated to the study of classical poetry and scorning sports. Two months after going up to Peterhouse, Cambridge, Gray sent this poem to Walpole, writing in his letter: 'I (tho' I say it) had too much modesty to venture answering your dear, diverting Letter, in the Poetical Strain myself: but, when I was last at the DEVIL, meeting by chance with the deceased Mr Dennis there, he offer'd his Service, &, being tip'd with a Tester, wrought, what follows –'

John Dennis, a dramatist, critic, and occasional poet, who had been satirized by Alexander Pope in the *Dunciad*, had died earlier that year. Atropos, in the third line, was the Greek Fate who cut the thread of life. Nicolino Grimaldi was an Italian opera-singer. The actress Anne Oldfield was well known for her liaisons with public figures. Artemisia, mentioned in the closing lines of the poem, was supposed daily to have mixed ashes in her drink to express her grief over her husband's death; here she drinks bohea, a tea. A ramilie is a wig.

[LINES SPOKEN BY THE GHOST OF JOHN DENNIS AT THE DEVIL TAVERN]

From purling Streams and the Elysian scene,
From groves that smile with never-fading green,
I reascend: in Atropos' despite
Restored to Celadon and upper light.
Ye gods, that sway the regions under ground,
Reveal to mortal view your realms profound;
At his command admit the eye of day:
When Celadon commands, what god can disobey?
Nor seeks he your Tartarean fires to know,
The house of torture and th'abyss of woe;
But happy fields and mansions free from pain,
Gay meads and springing flowers best please the gentle swain.

That little, naked, melancholy thing,
My soul, when first she tried her flight to wing,
Began with speed new regions to explore,
And blundered through a narrow postern door.
First most devoutly having said its prayers,
It tumbled down a thousand pair of stairs,

31

Through entries long, through cellars vast and deep,
Where ghostly rats their habitations keep,
Where spiders spread their webs and owlish goblins sleep.
After so many chances had befell,
It came into a mead of asphodel:
Betwixt the confines of the light and dark
It lies, of 'Lizium the St James's Park.
Here spirit-beaux flutter along the Mall,
And shadows in disguise skate o'er the iced canal;
Here groves embowered and more sequestered shades,
Frequented by the ghosts of ancient maids,
Are seen to rise. The melancholy scene,
With gloomy haunts and twilight walks between,
Conceals the wayward band: here spend their time
Greensickness girls that died in youthful prime,
Virgins forlorn, all dressed in willow-green-i
With Queen Elizabeth and Nicolini.

More to reveal, or many words to use,
Would tire alike your patience and my muse.
Believe that never was so faithful found
Queen Proserpine to Pluto under ground,
Or Cleopatra to her Mark Antony,
As Orozmades to his Celadony.

P.S. Lucrece for half a crown will show you fun,
But Mrs Oldfield is become a nun.
Nobles and cits, Prince Pluto and his spouse
Flock to the ghost of Covent-Garden House:
Plays, which were hissed above, below revive,
When dead applauded that were damned alive.
The people, as in life, still keep their passions,
But differ something from the world in fashions.
Queen Artemisia breakfasts on bohea,
And Alexander wears a ramilie.

Aged 17

William Collins
1721-1759

Joseph Warton tells that his friend Collins 'wrote his Eclogues when he was about seventeen years old, at Winchester School, and, as I well remember, had just been reading that volume of Salmon's Modern History, which described Persia; which determined him to lay the scene of these pieces [there]'. He also revealed that Collins, in later life, 'was accustomed to speak very contemptuously' of his Eclogues, and was distressed that they had found more readers and admirers than his Odes.

PERSIAN ECLOGUE THE SECOND

HASSAN; OR, THE CAMEL-DRIVER

SCENE, the Desert
TIME, Mid-day

In silent horror o'er the desert-waste
The driver Hassan with his camels passed.
One cruse of water on his back he bore,
And his light scrip contained a scanty store;
A fan of painted feathers in his hand,
To guard his shaded face from scorching sand.
The sultry sun had gained the middle sky,
And not a tree and not an herb was nigh.
The beasts with pain their dusty way pursue,
Shrill roared the winds and dreary was the view!
With desperate sorrow wild, the affrighted man
Thrice sighed, thrice struck his breast, and thus began:
  'Sad was the hour and luckless was the day,
  When first from Shiraz' walls I bent my way.

  'Ah! little thought I of the blasting wind,
The thirst or pinching hunger that I find!
Bethink thee, Hassan, where shall thirst assuage,
When fails this cruse, his unrelenting rage?
Soon shall this scrip its precious load resign,
Then what but tears and hunger shall be thine?

  'Ye mute companions of my toils, that bear
In all my griefs a more than equal share!
Here, where no springs in murmurs break away,

Or moss-crowned fountains mitigate the day,
In vain ye hope the green delights to know,
Which plains more blest or verdant vales bestow.
Here rocks alone and tasteless sands are found,
And faint and sickly winds for ever howl around.
    Sad was the hour and luckless was the day,
    When first from Schiraz' walls I bent my way.

    'Cursed be the gold and silver which persuade
Weak men to follow far-fatiguing trade.
The Lily-Peace outshines the silver store,
And life is dearer than the golden ore.
Yet money tempts us o'er the desert brown,
To every distant mart and wealthy town:
Full oft we tempt the land and oft the sea;
And are we only yet repaid by thee?
Ah! why was ruin so attractive made,
Or why fond man so easily betrayed?
Why heed we not, whilst mad we haste along,
The gentle voice of Peace or Pleasure's song?
Or wherefore think the flowery mountain's side,
The fountain's murmurs and the valley's pride,
Why think we these less pleasing to behold
Than dreary deserts, if they lead to gold?
    Sad was the hour and luckless was the day,
    When first from Schiraz' walls I bent my way.

    'O cease, my fears! all frantic as I go,
When thought creates unnumbered scenes of woe,
What if the lion in his rage I meet!
Oft in the dust I view his printed feet:
And fearful! oft, when Day's declining light
Yields her pale empire to the mourner Night,
By hunger roused, he scours the groaning plain,
Gaunt wolves and sullen tigers in his train:
Before them death with shrieks directs their way,
Fills the wild yell and leads them to their prey.
    Sad was the hour and luckless was the day,
    When first from Schiraz' walls I bent my way!

    'At that dead hour the silent asp shall creep,
If aught of rest I find, upon my sleep;
Or some swoll'n serpent twist his scales around,

34

And wake to anguish with a burning wound.
Thrice happy they, the wise contented poor,
From lust of wealth and dread of death secure.
They tempt no deserts and no griefs they find;
Peace rules the day, where reason rules the mind.
  Sad was the hour and luckless was the day,
  When first from Schiraz' walls I bent my way.

'O hapless youth! for she thy love hath won,
The tender Zara, will be most undone!
Big swelled my heart and owned the powerful maid,
When fast she dropped her tears, as thus she said:
"Farewell the youth whom sighs could not detain,
"Whom Zara's breaking heart implored in vain;
"Yet as thou goest, may every blast arise,
"Weak and unfelt as these rejected sighs!
"Safe o'er the wild, no perils mayst thou see,
"No griefs endure, nor weep, false youth, like me."
O let me safely to the fair return,
Say with a kiss, she must not, shall not mourn.
Go teach my heart to lose its painful fears,
Recalled by Wisdom's voice and Zara's tears.'

He said, and called on heaven to bless the day,
When back to Schiraz' walls he bent his way.

Aged 17

Christopher Smart
1722-1771

'His eldest sister Margaret [wrote Smart's younger daughter to a friend]
...has often repeated to me his first essay at numbers when about...4
years old...The young rhymester was very fond of a lady about three
times his own age who used to notice and caress him. A gentleman old
enough to be her father to teaze the child would pretend to be in love
with his favourite and threatened to take her for his wife – "You are too
old," said little Smart; the rival answered, if that was an objection he
would send his son; he answered in verse as follows, addressing the
lady.'

Madam if you please
To hear such things as these.
Madam, I have a rival sad
And if you don't take my part it will make me mad.
He says he will send his son;
But if he does I will get me a gun.
Madam if you please to pity,
O poor Kitty, O poor Kitty!

Aged 4

Thomas Chatterton
1752-1770

When Chatterton was seven years old, he entered Colston's Hospital, the Bluecoat School of Bristol, for a commercial education. His years there were unhappy ones. 'He had been gloomy from the time he began to learn,' his sister later recollected, 'but we remarked that he was more cheerful after he began to write poetry. Some satirical pieces we saw soon after.' 'Sly Dick', one of the first of these satirical poems, seems to refer to one of his schoolmates at Colston.

SLY DICK

Sharp was the frost, the wind was high,
And sparkling stars bedecked the sky,
Sly Dick, in arts of cunning skilled,
Whose rapine all his pockets filled,
Had laid him down to take his rest
And soothe with sleep his anxious breast.
'Twas thus a dark infernal sprite
A native of the blackest night,
Portending mischief to devise
Upon Sly Dick he cast his eyes,
Then straight descends th'infernal sprite,
And in his chamber does alight:
In visions he before him stands,
And his attention he commands;
　　Thus spake the sprite: 'Hearken, my friend,
And to my counsels now attend,
Within the garret's spacious dome
There lies a well stored wealthy room,
Well stored with cloth and stockings too,
Which I suppose will do for you,
First from the cloth take thou a purse
For thee it will not be the worse –
A noble purse rewards thy pains,
A purse to hold thy filching gains;
Then, for the stockings, let them reeve
And not a scrap behind thee leave
Five bundles for a penny sell
And pence to thee will come pell-mell;
See it be done with speed and care.'
Thus spake the sprite and sunk in air.

When in the morn, with thoughts erect
Sly Dick did on his dream reflect;
Why faith, thinks he, 'tis something too,
It might – perhaps – it might – be true,
I'll go and see. Away he hies,
And to the garret quick he flies,
Enters the room, cuts up the clothes –
And after that reeves up the hose;
Then of the cloth he purses made
    Purses to hold his filching trade –
            *Caetera desunt**

Aged 11

* Latin for 'the rest is missing'.

William Blake
1757-1827

Blake began his apprenticeship as an engraver in 1773, at the age of sixteen. In 1783 fifty copies of his *Poetical Sketches* appeared, with an apologetic preface by a friend stressing the poet's youth and the demands of his profession:

> The following sketches were the production of untutored youth, commenced in his twelfth, and occasionally resumed by the author till his twentieth year; since which time, his talents having been wholly directed to the attainment of excellence in his profession, he has been deprived of the leisure requisite to such a revisal of these sheets, as might have rendered them less unfit to meet the public eye.

SONG

How sweet I roamed from field to field,
　And tasted all the summer's pride,
'Till I the prince of love beheld,
　Who in the sunny beams did glide!

He showed me lilies for my hair,
　And blushing roses for my brow;
He led me through his gardens fair,
　Where all his golden pleasures grow.

With sweet May dews my wings were wet,
　And Phœbus fired my vocal rage;
He caught me in his silken net,
　And shut me in his golden cage.

He loves to sit and hear me sing,
　Then, laughing, sports and plays with me;
Then stretches out my golden wing,
　And mocks my loss of liberty.

Aged 13?

Robert Burns
1759-1796

Nelly Kirkpatrick was the girl for whom Burns wrote his first poem. It
appears in his Commonplace Book entitled 'SONG'. – (*Tune* – 'I am a
Man Unmarried') and is preceded by a note which ends: 'For my own
part I never had the least thought or inclination of turning poet till I got
once heartily in Love, and then Rhyme and Song were, in a manner,
the spontaneous language of my heart.'

O once I loved a bonnie lass,
   An' aye I love her still,
An' whilst that virtue warms my breast
   I'll love my handsome Nell.

As bonnie lasses I hae seen,
   And mony full as braw,
But for a modest gracefu' mien
   The like I never saw.

A bonny lass I will confess,
   Is pleasant to the e'e,
But without some better qualities
   She's no a lass for me.

But Nelly's looks are blithe and sweet,
   And what is best of a',
Her reputation is complete,
   And fair without a flaw;

She dresses aye sae clean and neat,
   Both decent and genteel;
And then there's something in her gait
   Gars ony dress look weel.

A gaudy dress and gentle air
   May slightly touch the heart,
But it's innocence and modesty
   That polishes the dart.

'Tis this in Nelly pleases me,
  'Tis this enchants my soul;
For absolutely in my breast
  She reigns without control.

Aged 16

William Wordsworth
1770-1850

'The beautiful image with which this poem concludes,' Wordsworth told Isabella Fenwick, many years after its composition, 'suggested itself to me while I was resting in a boat along with my companions under the shade of a magnificent row of Sycamores, which then extended their branches from the promontory upon which stands the ancient, and at that time the more picturesque, Hall of Coniston, the seat of the Le Flemings from very early times. The Poem of which it was the conclusion was of many hundred lines, and contained thoughts and images most of which have been dispersed through my other writings.'

[EXTRACT

FROM THE CONCLUSION OF A POEM,
COMPOSED IN ANTICIPATION OF LEAVING SCHOOL]

Dear native regions, I foretell,
From what I feel at this farewell,
That, wheresoe'er my steps may tend,
And whensoe'er my course shall end,
If in that hour a single tie
Survive of local sympathy,
My soul will cast the backward view,
The longing look alone on you.

Thus, while the Sun sinks down to rest
Far in the regions of the west,
Though to the vale no parting beam
Be given, not one memorial gleam,
A lingering light he fondly throws
On the dear hills where first he rose.

Aged 16

Sir Walter Scott
1771-1832

J.G. Lockhart, in his *Life of Scott*, wrote that the young Walter's 'transla-
tions in verse from Horace and Virgil were often approved by Dr Adam.
One of these little pieces [a translation from Virgil], written in a weak
boyish scrawl, within pencilled marks still visible, had been carefully
preserved by his mother; it was found folded up in a cover, inscribed
by the old lady – "My Walter's first lines, 1782".'

In awful ruins Ætna thunders nigh,
And sends in pitchy whirlwinds to the sky
Black clouds of smoke, which still as they aspire,
From their dark sides there bursts the glowing fire;
At other times huge balls of fire are tossed,
That lick the stars, and in the smoke are lost;
Sometimes the mount, with vast convulsions torn,
Emits huge rocks, which instantly are borne
With loud explosions to the starry skies,
The stones made liquid as the huge mass flies,
Then back again with greater weight recoils,
While Ætna thundering from the bottom boils.

Aged 11

Walter Savage Landor
1775-1864

In 1795 Landor published his first book of poems, a publication he soon regretted. Only a few years later he commented: 'Before I was twenty years of age I had imprudently sent into the world a volume, of which I was soon ashamed. It every-where met with as much condemnation as was proper, and generally more. For, tho' the structure was feeble, the lines were fluent: the rhymes shewed habitual ease, and the personifications fashionable taste...'

'To a Lady Lately Married' is the earliest of the poems in that volume, written when Landor was still at Rugby. The lady he addresses is thought to be his cousin Sophia, who married John Shuckburgh of Bourton Hall in 1788.

TO A LADY LATELY MARRIED

I

From Pride's embraces and from Fortune's smiles
Few are the damsels that have power to fly:
   They, bound in Torpor's chilly toils,
     Struck by strong inchantment lie.

II

O'er thee, Sophia! Love alone presides;
O'er thee, I view his purple pinions play!
   Thus, fluttering on the vernal tides,
     Shines the lightsome rosy ray.

III

Blest! who from Fortune and from Pride hast fled
Where pure Affection's genial warmth persuades!
   Thy paths may tender Beauty tread,
     Paths where Pleasure never fades.

IV

Nor else the primrose, wet with early dew,
Closes her bosom from approaching Night:
   But glad the joyful Morn to view,
     Sips the lively stream of light.

Aged 14

Lord George Byron
1788-1824

Byron's friend and biographer, Thomas Moore, wrote:
It was about this period [1796], according to his nurse, May Gray, that the first symptom of any tendency towards rhyming showed itself in him; and the occasion which she represented as having given rise to this childish effort was as follows. An elderly lady, who was in the habit of visiting his mother, had made use of some expression that very much affronted him; and these slights, his nurse said, he generally resented violently and implacably. The old lady had some curious notions respecting the soul, which, she imagined, took its flight to the moon after death, as a preliminary essay before it proceeded further. One day, after a repetition, it is supposed of her original insult to the boy, he appeared before his nurse in a violent rage. 'Well, my little hero,' she asked, 'what's the matter with you now?' Upon which the child answered, that this old woman had put him in a 'most terrible passion – that he could not bear the sight of her,' etc., etc., – and then broke into the following doggerel, which he repeated over and over, as if delighted with the vent he had found for his rage:

In Nottingham county there lives at Swan Green,
As curst an old lady as ever was seen;
And when she does die, which I hope will be soon,
She firmly believes she will go to the moon.

Aged 8

Percy Bysshe Shelley
1792-1822

Shelley wrote the following verses for his sister Elizabeth at school. Commenting on the concluding stanza, their sister Hellen later recalled: 'That last expression is, I imagine, still *classical* at boy's schools, and it was a favourite one of Bysshe's, which I remember from a painful fact, that one of my sisters ventured to make use of it, and was punished in some old-fashioned way, which impressed the sentence on my memory.'

[VERSES ON A CAT]

A cat in distress,
Nothing more, or less;
Good folks, I must faithfully tell ye,
As I am a sinner,
It wants for some dinner
To stuff out its own little belly.

You'd not easily guess
All the modes of distress
Which torture the tenants of earth;
And the various evils,
Which like many devils,
Attend the poor dogs from their birth.

Some a living require,
And others desire
An old fellow out of the way;
And which is the best
I leave to be guessed,
For I cannot pretend to say.

One wants society,
Tother variety,
Others a tranquil life;
Some want food,
Others, as good,
Only require a wife.

But this poor little cat
Only wanted a rat,
To stuff out its own little maw;
And 'twere as good
Had some people such food,
To make them hold their jaw!

Aged 10

John Clare
1793-1864

Clare's boyhood was spent in north-east Northamptonshire, in the village of Helpston. Sundays he spent in the woods and fields, where he found particular delight in 'watching the habits of birds'. 'I grew so much into the quiet love of nature's preserves,' he later wrote in his *Autobiography*, 'that I was never easy but when I was in the fields.' 'The Robin', written when he was sixteen, describes a tame bird which he was to recollect in his *Natural History Letters* in 1824, observing the Robin's 'fondness for man':

> In winter it will venture into the house for food and become as tame as a chicken – we had one that used to come in at a broken pane in the window for three winters together I always knew it to be our old visitor by a white scar on one of the wings it grew so tame that it would perch on one's finger and take crumbs out of the hand it was very much startled at the cat at first but after a time it took little notice of her further than always contriving to keep out of her way – it would never stay in the house at night though it would attempt to perch on the chair spindles and clean its bill and ruffle its feathers and put its head under its wing as if it had made up its mind to stay but something or other always molested it when it suddenly sought its old broken pane and departed when it was sure to be the first riser in the morning.

THE ROBIN

Now the snow hides the ground, little birds leave the wood,
And fly to the cottage to beg for their food;
While the robin, domestic, more tame than the rest,
With its wings drooping down, and rough feathers undressed,
Comes close to our windows, as much as to say,
'I would venture in, if I could find a way:
I'm starved, and I want to get out of the cold;
Oh! make me a passage, and think me not bold.'
Ah, poor little creature! thy visits reveal
Complaints such as these to the heart that can feel;
Nor shall such complainings be urged in vain;
I'll make thee a hole, if I take out a pane.
Come in, and a welcome reception thou'lt find;
I keep no grimalkin to murder inclined.
But oh, little robin! be careful to shun
That house, where the peasant makes use of a gun;
For if thou but taste of the seed he has strewed,

Thy life as a ransom must pay for the food:
His aim is unerring, his heart is as hard,
And thy race, though so harmless, he'll never regard.
Distinction with him, boy, is nothing at all;
Both the wren, and the robin, with sparrows must fall.
For his soul (though he outwardly looks like a man)
Is in nature a wolf of the Apennine clan;
Like them his whole study is bent on his prey:
Then be careful, and shun what is meant to betray.
Come, come to my cottage, and thou shalt be free
To perch on my finger and sit on my knee:
Thou shalt eat of the crumbles of bread to thy fill,
And have leisure to clean both thy feathers and bill.
Then come, little robin! and never believe
Such warm invitations are meant to deceive:
In duty I'm bound to show mercy on thee,
Since God don't deny it to sinners like me.

Aged 16

John Keats
1795-1821

Although Keats left Clarke's School at the age of fourteen, he maintained a close friendship with Charles Cowden Clarke, the headmaster's son and a pupil-teacher at the school. They met several times a week, and Clarke provided his former pupil with ample reading. One evening early in the spring of 1814, Clarke read Spenser's *Epithalamion* aloud to the eighteen-year-old Keats, who was so delighted that he immediately departed with the first volume of the *Faerie Queen*. 'He ramped through' the book, Clarke later recollected, 'like a young horse turned into a Spring meadow.' Keats's 'Imitation of Spenser', thought by many to be his first poem, was the result.

IMITATION OF SPENSER

Now Morning from her orient chamber came,
And her first footsteps touched a verdant hill;
Crowning its lawny crest with amber flame,
Silv'ring the untainted gushes of its rill;
Which, pure from mossy beds, did down distill,
And after parting beds of simple flowers,
By many streams a little lake did fill,
Which round its marge reflected woven bowers,
And, in its middle space, a sky that never lowers.

There the king-fisher saw his plumage bright
Vieing with fish of brilliant dye below;
Whose silken fins, and golden scales light
Cast upward, through the waves, a ruby glow:
There saw the swan his neck of archéd snow,
And oared himself along with majesty;
Sparkled his jetty eyes; his feet did show
Beneath the waves like Afric's ebony,
And on his back a fay reclined voluptuously.

Ah! I could tell the wonders of an isle
That in that fairest lake had placéd been,
I could e'en Dido of her grief beguile;
Or rob from aged Lear his bitter teen:
For sure so fair a place was never seen,
Of all that ever charmed romantic eye:
It seemed an emerald in the silver sheen

Of the bright waters; or as when on high,
Through clouds of fleecy white, laughs the cœrulean sky.

And all around it dipped luxuriously
Slopings of verdure through the glassy tide,
Which, as it were in gentle amity,
Rippled delighted up the flowery side;
As if to glean the ruddy tears, it tried,
Which fell profusely from the rose-tree stem!
Haply it was the workings of its pride,
In strife to throw upon the shore a gem
Outvieing all the buds in Flora's diadem.

Aged 18

Thomas Lovell Beddoes
1803-1849

In June 1817, Beddoes entered Charterhouse School in London, where he soon amused his classmates by penning lurid tragedies and tales of terror. A comet visible over London for several nights prompted his first published poem, in which he depicts the comet as an emissary of Yamen, the Hindu god of fire.

THE COMET

The eye of the demon on Albion was turned,
And, viewing the happy, with envy he burned;
He snarled at the churches, the almshouse he cursed,
Till hate of their virtue his silence had burst:
'Why waves yonder harvest? why glitters yon tower?
'My hate they despise, and they scoff at my power.
'Then lend me assistance, ye elements dire,
'Attend at my call, air, earth, water, and fire.'
He spoke; and, lo! pregnant with flame and with pest,
The scorch of the blast his rough mandate confessed,
The flame of the typhus, the stifling damp,
And there rode the blast that will smother the lamp.
'In vain you command us; the heart-easing prayer,
'And the sounds of the hymn, as they wind through the air,
'Blunt the arrows of sickness which pestilence bear.'

Then loud was the roar as the wind fled away;
Till earth trembled and spoke from the regions of day;
'The shocks of my mountains roll cataracts back,
'And from north to the south could the universe crack,
'But the heart of the ocean I may not attack.'

The thunder was o'er ànd the motion was still,
But the god of the waters thus murmured his will;
'All Europe my waves in a moment shall hide,
'And the old world, and new, be swallowed by tide,
'But the Albion isle shall my prowess deride.'

The waves had sunk down, and the billows were hushed,
Ere the flame of destruction before him had rushed;
'Whole cities and empires have died at my blast,
'So strong is my power, my rapine so fast:
'But Britain, unhurt, shall endure to the last.'

In vain frowned the demon, 'Still terror I'll try,
'And the envoy of Yamen shall fleet through your sky.'
But while virtue and justice in Britain remain,
The fire-brand of Yamen shall dazzle in vain.

Aged 15

Elizabeth Barrett Browning
1806-1861

It is said that Elizabeth Barrett wrote her first poem in her sixth year, and for some lines on 'Virtue' carefully written out, received from her father a ten-shilling note enclosed in a letter addressed to the *Poet Laureate of Hope End*.

A later poem gives a vivid impression of daily life at Hope End.

To school till five! and then again we fly
To play and joy and mirth and pleasures ply.
Some dance, some fight, some laugh, some play, some squall,
And the loud organ's thunder circles all.
And then at tea we snatch a short repast
As long as one large plate of toast doth last.
At nine fatigued upon the grateful bed
We stretch out weary limbs and rest our head.

Aged 13

Edgar Allan Poe
1809-1849

At fourteen, Poe was writing verses to girls, but it was a visit to the home of a schoolfriend, Robert Stannard, that inspired the finest of his early poems: 'Mrs Stannard was in one of the front rooms standing by a window niche. The light falling upon her, caught in her dark ringlets crossed by a white snood, glowed in the classic folds of her gown, and flowed about her slenderly graceful figure.'

TO HELEN

Helen, thy beauty is to me
   Like those Nicéan barks of yore,
That gently, o'er a perfumed sea,
   The weary, way-worn wanderer bore
   To his own native shore.

On desperate seas long wont to roam,
   Thy hyacinth hair, thy classic face,
Thy Naiad airs have brought me home
   To the glory that was Greece,
   And the grandeur that was Rome.

Lo! in yon brilliant window-niche
   How statue-like I see thee stand,
The agate lamp within thy hand!
   Ah, Psyche, from the regions which
   Are Holy-Land!

Aged 15/16

Alfred Lord Tennyson
1809-1892

Tennyson remembered having first been moved by poetry at the age of five, and by his own account, he began composing verses at eight:

> According to the best of my recollection, when I was about eight years old, I covered two sides of a slate with Thomsonian blank verse in praise of flowers, for my brother Charles, who was a year older than I was, Thomson then being the only poet I knew. ... About ten or eleven, Pope's *Homer's Iliad* became a favourite of mine and I wrote hundreds and hundreds of lines in the regular Popeian metre, nay even could improvise them, so could my two elder brothers, for my father was a poet and could write metre very skillfully. ... At about twelve and onward I wrote an epic of six thousand lines à la Walter Scott with Scott's regularity of octosyllables and his occasional varieties. Though the performance was very likely worth nothing I never felt myself more truly inspired, I wrote as much as seventy lines at one time, and used to go shouting them about the fields after dark.

In 1827, Alfred and Charles Tennyson published *Poems by Two Brothers*, for which the publishers paid them one hundred pounds.

MEMORY

Memory! dear enchanter!
　Why bring back to view
Dreams of youth, which banter
　All that e'er was true?

Why present before me
　Thoughts of years gone by,
Which, like shadows o'er me,
　Dim in distance fly?

Days of youth, now shaded
　By twilight of long years,
Flowers of youth, now faded,
　Though bathed in sorrow's tears:

Thoughts of youth, which waken
　Mournful feelings now,
Fruits which time hath shaken
　From off their parent bough:

Memory! why, oh why,
    This fond heart consuming,
Show me years gone by,
    When those hopes were blooming?

Hopes which now are parted,
    Hopes which then I prized,
Which this world, cold-hearted,
    Ne'er has realized?

I knew not then its strife,
    I knew not then its rancour;
In every rose of life,
    Alas! there lurks a canker.

Round every palm-tree, springing
    With bright fruit in the waste,
A mournful asp is clinging,
    Which sours it to our taste.

O'er every fountain, pouring
    Its waters through the wild,
Which man imbibes, adoring,
    And deems it undefiled,

The poison-shrubs are dropping
    Their dark dews day by day;
And Care is hourly lopping
    Our greenest boughs away!

Ah! these are thoughts that grieve me
    Then, when others rest.
Memory! why deceive me
    By thy visions blest?

Why lift the veil, dividing
    The brilliant courts of spring –
Where gilded shapes are gliding
    In fairy colouring –

From age's frosty mansion,
    So cheerless and so chill?
Why did the bleak expansion
    Of past life meet us still?

Where's now that peace of mind
　　O'er youth's pure bosom stealing,
So sweet and so refined,
　　So exquisite a feeling?

Where's now the heart exulting
　　In pleasure's buoyant sense,
And gaiety, resulting
　　From conscious innocence?

All, all have past and fled,
　　And left me lorn and lonely;
All those dear hopes are dead,
　　Remembrance wakes them only!

I stand like some lone tower
　　Of former days remaining,
Within whose place of power
　　The midnight owl is plaining; –

Like oak-tree old and grey,
　　Whose trunk with age is failing,
Through whose dark boughs for aye
　　The winter winds are wailing.

Thus, Memory, thus thy light
　　O'er this worn soul is gleaming,
Like some far fire at night
　　Along the dun deep streaming.

Aged 17?

58

Robert Browning
1812-1889

In 'The Dance of Death', an ambitious poem of 103 lines written when Browning was fourteen, he imagines Fever, Madness, Consumption, Pestilence, Ague as figures dancing in a circle, each in turn singing that *it* is the most deadly enemy of mankind. Here are the first two songs.

from THE DANCE OF DEATH

And as they footed it around,
They sang their triumphs o'er mankind!

de Stael.

FEVER

Bow to me, bow to me;
Follow me in my burning breath,
Which brings as the simoom destruction and death.
My spirit lives in the hectic glow
When I bid the life streams tainted flow
In the fervid sun's deep brooding beam
When seething vapours in volumes steam,
And they fall – the young, the gay – as the flower
'Neath the fiery wind's destructive power.
This day I have gotten a noble prize –
There was one who saw the morning rise,
And watched fair Cynthia's golden streak
Kiss the misty mountain peak,
But I was there, and my pois'nous flood
Envenomed the gush of the youth's warm blood.
They hastily bore him to his bed,
But o'er him death his swart pennons spread:
The skilléd leech's art was vain,
Delirium revelled in each vein.

MADNESS

Hear ye not the gloomy yelling
Or the tide of anguish swelling,
Hear the clank of fetter and chain,
Hear ye the wild cry of grief and pain,
Followed by the shuddering laugh

As when fiends the life blood quaff?
See! see that band,
See how their bursting eyeballs gleam,
As the tiger's when crouched in the jungle's lair,
In India's sultry land.
Now they are seized in the rabies fell,
Hark! 'tis a shriek as from fiends of hell;
Now there is a plaining moan,
As the flow of the sullen river –
List! there is a hollow groan.
Doth it not make e'en *you* to shiver –
These are they struck of the barbs of my quiver.
Slaves before my haughty throne,
Bow then, bow to me alone.

Aged 14

Charlotte Brontë
1816-1855

Charlotte Brontë wrote more than half of her poetry between the ages of thirteen and twenty. Only a few years later she looked back on her career with somewhat precocious maturity:

> Once indeed I was very poetical, when I was sixteen, seventeen, eighteen and nineteen years old – but I am now twenty-four approaching twenty-five – and the intermediate years are those which begin to rob life of its superfluous coloring. At this age it is time that the imagination should be pruned and trimmed – that the judgment should be cultivated – and a *few* at least, of the countless illusions of early youth should be cleared away. I have not written poetry for a long while.

Such repudiations were not uncharacteristic. Charlotte Brontë's earliest known poem was 'The Song of the Fairies', written when she was thirteen. After a year at school, she called her fairies and genii together in their aerial palace over the city of Verdopolis to dismiss them. They were not to return to her poems or stories thereafter.

THE FAIRIES' FAREWELL

The trumpet hath sounded, its voice is gone forth
From the plains of the south to the seas of the north;
The great ocean groaned, and the firm mountains shook,
And the rivers in terror their channels forsook.
The proud eagle quailed in her aerial dome,
The gentle dove flew to her bowery home,
The antelope trembled as onward she sprang,
When hollow and death-like the trumpet-blast rang.

It was midnight, deep midnight, and shrouded in sleep
Men heard not the roar of the terror-struck deep
Nor the peal of the trumpet still sounding on high;
They saw not the flashes that brightened the sky.
All silent and tomb-like the great city lay,
And fair rose her towers in their moonlight array:
'Twas the Ruler of Spirits that sent forth the sound
To call his dread legions in myriads around.

They heard him, and from land and wave
    The genii armies sprung:
Some came from dim green ocean cave
    Where thousand gems are flung;

Some from the forests of the west,
    'Mid dark shades wandering;
A giant host of wingéd forms
    Rose round their mighty king!

Some from the chill and ice-bound north,
    All swathed in snowy shrouds,
With the wild howl of storms came forth
    Sailing in tempest-clouds.

The gentler fays in bright bands flew
    From each sweet woodland dell,
All broidered with the violet blue,
    And wild-flower's drooping bell.

A sound of harps was on the blast
    Breathing faint melody;
A dim light was from distance cast
    As their fair troops drew nigh.

And, mingling with stern giant forms,
    Their tiny shapes are seen,
Bright gleaming 'mid the gloom of storms
    Their gems and robes of green.

The Hall where they sat was the heart of the sky,
And the stars to give light stooped their lamps from on high.
The noise of the host rose like thunder around,
The heavens gathered gloom at the grave sullen sound.
No mortal may farther the vision reveal:
Human eye cannot pierce what a spirit would seal.
The secrets of genii my tongue may not tell,
But hoarsely they murmured: 'Bright city, farewell!'
Then melted away like a dream of the night,
While their palace evanished in oceans of light.
Far beneath them the city lay silent and calm;
The breath of the night-wind was softer than balm
As it sighed o'er its gardens, and mourned in its bowers,

And shook the bright dew-drops from orient flowers;
But still as the breeze on the myrtle-groves fell,
A voice was heard wailing: 'Bright city, farewell!'
The morning rose over the far distant hill,
And yet the great city lay silent and still.
No chariot rode thunderous adown the wide street,
No horse of Arabia, impetuous and fleet.
The river flowed on to the foam-crested sea,
But, unburdened by vessel, its waves murmured free.
The silence is dreadful. O city, arise!
The sound is ascending the arch of the skies.
Mute, mute are the mighty, and chilled is their breath,
For at midnight passed o'er them the Angel of Death!
The king and the peasant, the lord and the slave,
Lie entombed in the depth of one wide solemn grave.

Aged 15

Emily Brontë
1818-1848

When Charlotte, oldest of the four Brontë children, went away to school, her sisters Emily and Anne began to write stories and poems about the loves and feuds of the inhabitants of Gondal, an imaginary island in the Pacific Ocean. Their prose has been lost, but almost two hundred of Emily's poems survive. In this one, Augusta Geraldine Almeda addresses Alexander, Lord of Elbë, the lover who years before had died of wounds received in battle, his head pillowed in her lap.

A.G.A. TO A.E.

Lord of Elbë, on Elbë hill
The mist is thick and the wind is chill
And the heart of thy Friend from the dawn of day
Has sighed for sorrow that thou went away.

Lord of Elbë, how pleasant to me
The sound of thy blithesome step would be
Rustling the heath that, only now
Waves as the night-gusts over it blow.

Bright are the fires in thy lonely home
I see them far off, and as deepens the gloom
Gleaming like stars through the high forest-boughs
Gladder they glow in the park's repose.

O Alexander! when I return,
Warm as those hearths my heart would burn,
Light as thine own, my foot would fall
If I might hear thy voice in the hall.

But thou art now on desolate sea –
Parted from Gondal and parted from me –
All my repining is hopeless and vain,
Death never yields back his victims again.

Aged 19

Arthur Hugh Clough
1819-1861

One day, when Clough was lying in the sick-room of the School House at Rugby, he saw the younger children of the headmaster, Dr Arnold, playing in the garden below, and wrote the following poem, addressed to their father.

THOUGHTS OF HOME

I watched them from the window, thy children at their play,
And I thought of all my own dear friends, who were far, oh! far
    away,
And childish loves, and childish cares, and a child's own buoyant
    gladness
Came gushing back again to me with a soft and solemn sadness,
And feelings frozen up full long, and thoughts of long ago,
Seemed to be thawing at my heart with a warm and sudden glow.

I looked upon thy children, and I thought of all and each,
Of my brother and my sister, and our rambles on the beach,
Of my mother's gentle voice, and my mother's beckoning hand,
And all the tales she used to tell of the far, far English land;
And the happy, happy evening hours when I sat on my father's
    knee, –
Oh! many a wave is rolling now betwixt that seat and me!

And many a day has passed away since I left them o'er the sea,
And I have lived a life since then of boyhood's thoughtless glee,
Yet of the blessed times gone by not seldom would I dream,
And childhood's joy, like faint far stars, in memory's heaven
    would gleam,
And o'er the sea to those I loved my thoughts would often roam,
But never knew I until now the blessings of a home!

I used to think when I was there that my own true home was
    here, –
But home is not in land or sky, but in those whom each holds dear;
The evening's cooling breeze is fanning my temples now,
But then my frame was languid and heated was my brow,
And I longed for England's cool, and for England's breezes then,
But now I would give full many a breeze to be back in the heat
    again.

But when cold strange looks without, and proud high thoughts
    within,
Are weaving round my heart the woof of selfishness and sin,
When self begins to roll a far, a worse and wider sea
Of careless and unloving thoughts between those friends and me,
I will think upon these moments, and call to mind the day
When I watched them from the window, thy children at their play.

Aged 16

Christina Rossetti
1830-1894

Rossetti composed her first story, 'The Dervise', when she was still too young to write, and her first poem was dictated to her mother:

> Cecilia never went to school
> Without her gladiator.

When she was eleven years old she presented two quatrains to her mother for her birthday, earning the prediction that Christina would be 'the poet of the family'. She wrote 'The Chinaman' in competition with her brother William, whose school assignment was to write some verses on the Anglo-Chinese Opium War of 1842.

THE CHINAMAN

'Centre of Earth!' a Chinaman he said,
And bent over a map his pig-tailed head, –
That map in which, portrayed in colours bright,
China, all dazzling, burst upon the sight;
'Centre of Earth!' repeatedly he cries,
'Land of the brave, the beautiful, the wise!'
Thus he exclaimed; when lo his words arrested
Showed what sharp agony his head had tested.
He feels a tug – another, and another –
And quick exclaims, 'Hallo! what's now the bother?'
But soon, alas, perceives. And, 'Why, false night,
Why not from men shut out the hateful sight?
The faithless English have cut off my tail,
And left me my sad fortunes to bewail.
Now in the streets I can no more appear,
For all the other men a pig-tail wear.'
He said, and furious cast into the fire
His tail: those flames became its funeral-pyre.

Aged 11

Emily Dickinson
1830-1886

'I am growing handsome very fast indeed!' Emily wrote to a school friend when she was fourteen years old, 'I expect to be the belle of Amherst when I reach my 17th year.' Though never quite a belle, she was soon to attract many friends and admirers. The winter of 1849 provided a merry round of parties, charades, suppers, sociables, and sleigh rides. She also participated in the winter custom of exchanging Valentines, penning a somewhat morbid verse ('Life is but a strife') illustrated with magazine clippings for her friend William Cowper Dickinson, and an exuberantly satiric prose Valentine, published in February in the Amherst College *Indicator*, which opened: 'Magnum bonum, "harum scarum," zounds et zounds, et war alarum, man reformam, life perfectum, mundum changum, all things flarum?' On 4 March she composed a somewhat more conventional Valentine for Elbridge Bowdoin, a partner in her father's law office, in which she counselled the twenty-nine-year-old bachelor to choose a wife among the six 'comely maidens' who surrounded him: Sarah Taylor, Eliza Coleman, Emeline Kellog, Harriet Merrill, Susan Gilbert, and Emily herself ('she with *curling hair*'). Mr Bowdoin was unswayed; he remained a bachelor for the rest of his life. But he preserved Emily's Valentine for forty years.

[A VALENTINE]

Awake ye muses nine, sing me a strain divine,
Unwind the solemn twine, and tie my Valentine!

Oh the Earth was *made* for lovers, for damsel, and hopeless swain,
For sighing, and gentle whispering, and *unity* made of *twain*.
All things do go a courting, in earth, or sea, or air,
God hath made nothing single but *thee* in His world so fair!
The *bride*, and then the *bridegroom*, the *two*, and then the *one*,
Adam, and Eve, his consort, the moon, and then the sun;
The life doth prove the precept, who obey shall happy be,
Who will not serve the sovereign, be hanged on fatal tree.
The high do seek the lowly, the great do seek the small,
None cannot find who *seeketh*, on this terrestrial ball;
The bee doth court the flower, the flower his suit receives,
And they make merry wedding, whose guests are hundred leaves;
The wind doth woo the branches, the branches they are won,
And the father fond demandeth the maiden for his son.
The storm doth walk the seashore humming a mournful tune,
The wave with eye so pensive, looketh to see the moon,

Their spirits meet together, they make them solemn vows,
No more he singeth mournful, her sadness she doth lose.
The *worm* doth woo the *mortal*, death claims a living bride,
Night unto day is married, morn unto eventide;
Earth is a merry damsel, and *heaven* a knight so true,
And Earth is quite coquettish, and beseemeth in vain to sue.
Now to the *application*, to the reading of the roll,
To bringing thee to justice, and marshalling thy soul:
Thou art a *human* solo, a being cold, and lone,
Wilt have no kind companion, thou *reap'st* what thou hast *sown*.
Hast never silent hours, and minutes all too long,
And a deal of sad reflection, and *wailing* instead of song?
There's *Sarah*, and *Eliza*, and *Emeline* so fair,
And *Harriet*, and *Susan*, and she with *curling hair*!
Thine eyes are sadly blinded, but yet thou mayest see
Six true, and comely maidens sitting upon the tree;
Approach that tree with caution, then up it boldly climb,
And seize the one thou lovest, nor care for *space*, or *time*!
Then bear her to the greenwood, and build for her a bower,
And give her what she asketh, jewel, or bird, or flower –
And bring the fife, and trumpet, and beat upon the drum –
And bid the world Goodmorrow, and go to glory home!

Aged 19

Algernon Swinburne
1837-1909

One of Swinburne's earliest poetic efforts was a four-act verse drama in the style of Cyril Tourneur, whom he had admired, he later said, from the 'ripe age of twelve'. In a letter to John Churton Collins in December 1876, he recalled his youthful enthusiasm:

> ...I first read *The Revenger's Tragedy* in my tutor's Dodsley at Eton (which he was actually kind enough to entrust to such a small boy) with infinite edification, and such profit that to the utter neglect of my school work..., I forthwith wrote a tragedy of which I have utterly forgotten the very name (having had the sense at sixteen to burn it together with every other scrap of MS. I had in the world), but into which I do remember that, with ingenuity worthy of a better cause, I had contrived to pack twice as many rapes and about three times as many murders as are contained in the model, which is not noticeably or exceptionally deficient in such incident. It must have been a sweet work, and full of the tender and visionary innocence of childhood's unsullied fancy.

The play was *The Unhappy Revenge*, and Swinburne evidently did not have the sense to burn it at sixteen. His biographer Philip Henderson notes that in fact the play actually contains 'only one rape, one suicide, two murders by poison and four executions, though it is unfinished and the final act would have provided an opportunity for further horrors.' The following extracts are speeches made by the Christian martyr Eroclea and her father, before they die by torture:

> What is that death they boast but a frail pageant,
> A shade that falls and passes? 'Tis a cloud
> That but dissolves in rain, sweet Nature's tears,
> And leaves a rainbow, shaded with each hue,
> Of varying light, to make a blessed arch
> That opens our way to Heaven.

*

>   Thank your engines;
> They have drawn down heaven upon me. I am torn
> From Life to happiness: when I wear my crown,
> I'll pray it may be yours. When I am gone,
> Witness your rack for me, I forced you not;

No sea of glass sustained my withered frame;
My soul grows bright with shadows of the past
Dissolved; I am released; farewell; this death
Is more than life to me.

Aged 12

Thomas Hardy
1840-1928

In this, his first surviving poem, Hardy remembers his grandmother, one of the most important figures of his childhood talking of her life when first she came to live in her newly-built house at Higher Brockhampton in Dorset.

DOMICILIUM

It faces west, and round the back and sides
High beeches, bending, hang a veil of boughs,
And sweep against the roof. Wild honeysucks
Climb on the walls, and seem to sprout a wish
(If we may fancy wish of trees and plants)
To overtop the apple-trees hard by.

Red roses, lilacs, variegated box
Are there in plenty, and such hardy flowers
As flourish best untrained. Adjoining these
Are herbs and esculents; and farther still
A field; then cottages with trees, and last
The distant hills and sky.

Behind, the scene is wilder. Heath and furze
Are everything that seems to grow and thrive
Upon the uneven ground. A stunted thorn
Stands here and there, indeed; and from a pit
An oak uprises, springing from a seed
Dropped by some bird a hundred years ago.

                    In days bygone –
Long gone – my father's mother, who is now
Blest with the blest, would take me out to walk.
At such a time I once inquired of her
How looked the spot when first she settled here.
The answer I remember. 'Fifty years
Have passed since then, my child, and change has marked
The face of all things. Yonder garden-plots
And orchards were uncultivated slopes
O'ergrown with bramble bushes, furze and thorn:
That road a narrow path shut in by ferns,
Which, almost trees, obscured the passer-by.

'Our house stood quite alone, and those tall firs
And beeches were not planted. Snakes and efts
Swarmed in the summer days, and nightly bats
Would fly about our bedrooms. Heathcroppers
Lived on the hills, and were our only friends;
So wild it was when first we settled here.'

Aged 17

Oscar Wilde
1854-1900

When Isola Francesca Wilde died in 1867, at the age of eight, her twelve-year-old brother Oscar was heart-broken. He made long and frequent visits to her grave, and some years later wrote this poem.

REQUIESCAT

Tread lightly, she is near
  Under the snow,
    Speak gently, she can hear
The daisies grow.

All her bright golden hair
  Tarnished with rust,
She that was young and fair
  Fallen to dust.

Lily-like, white as snow,
  She hardly knew
She was a woman, so
  Sweetly she grew.

Coffin-board, heavy stone
  Lie on her breast,
I vex my heart alone,
  She is at rest.

Peace, Peace, she cannot hear
  Lyre or sonnet,
All my life's buried here,
  Heap earth upon it.

Amy Lowell
1874-1925

In the spring of 1883, Amy Lowell was taken on a cross-country tour from her native Massachusetts to the West Coast. At the urging of her parents, she kept a journal. Her first poem, 'Chacago', follows the final entry in *Notes of my trip to and from California*.

CHACAGO

Chacago. ditto
the land of
the free.
It is on lake
Mich'gan, and
not on the sea.
It has some
fine houses
in the suberbs
I'm told
And its people
are rolling in
silver and
gold.
In the city
it'self there
are
warehouses
large.
The folks go
on the lake
in sail boat
and barge.
But for all
of its ~~beauty~~
I'de rather
go home.
To Boston,
Charles River,
and the
State houses
dome.

Aged 9

Robert Frost
1874-1963

Frost said that the first poem he ever wrote was 'La Noche Triste' (Spanish for 'The Sad Night'). Based on a story he had found in William Hickling Prescott's book, *The Conquest of Mexico*, it describes a battle between the Aztec Indians and the Spaniards, under their leader, Cortez.

Montezuma II (1466-1520), the last Aztec Emperor, had welcomed Cortez and his men to his capital, Tenochtitlan (literally 'Place of the High Priest Tenoch'), but a week later Cortez took Montezuma captive. After six months, the Aztecs revolted, Montezuma was killed, the Spaniards destroyed the Aztecs' great Temple, and were then forced to retreat over a narrow causeway besieged by Aztec warriors in canoes.

LA NOCHE TRISTE

TENOCHTITLAN

Changed is the scene: the peace
And regal splendor which
Once that city knew are gone,
And war now reigns upon
That throng, who but
A week ago were all
Intent on joy supreme.
Cries of the wounded break
The stillness of the night,
Or challenge of the guard.
The Spaniard many days
Beseiged within the place,
Where kings did rule of old,
Now pressed by hunger by
The all-relentless foe,
Looks for some channel of
Escape. The night is dark;
Black clouds obscure the sky –
A dead calm lies o'er all.
The heart of one is firm,
His mind is constant still,
To all, his word is law.
Cortes his plan hath made,
The time hath come. Each one
His chosen place now takes,

There waits the signal, that
Will start the long retreat.

THE FLIGHT

Anon the cry comes down the line,
The portals wide are swung,
A long dark line moves out the gate,
And now the flight's begun.

Aye, cautiously it moves at first,
As ship steered o'er the reef,
Looking for danger all unseen,
But which may bring to grief.

Straight for the causeway now they make,
The bridge is borne before,
'Tis ta'en and placed across the flood,
And all go trooping o'er.

Yet e'er the other side is reached,
Wafted along the wind,
The rolling of the snake-skin drum
Comes floating from behind.

And scarcely has its rolling ceased,
Than out upon the lake,
Where all was silence just before,
A conch the calm doth break.

What terror to each heart it bears,
That sound of ill portent,
Each gunner to escape now looks,
On safety all are bent.

Forward they press in wild despair,
On to the next canal,
Held on all sides by foe and sea,
Like deer within corral.

Now surging this way, now in that,
The mass sways to and fro,
The infidel around it sweeps –
Slowly the night doth go.

A war cry soundeth through the night,
The 'tzin! the 'tzin! is there,
His plume nods wildly o'er the scene,
Oh, Spaniard, now beware!

With gaping jaws the cannon stands,
Points it among the horde;
The valiant Leon waits beside,
Ready with match and sword.

The 'tzin quick springeth to his side,
His mace he hurls on high,
It crasheth through the Spanish steel,
And Leon prone doth lie.

Falling, he died beneath his gun, –
He died at duty's call,
And many falling on that night,
Dying, so died they all.

The faithful guarders at the bridge,
Have worked with might and main,
Nor can they move it from its place,
Swollen by damp of rain.

On through the darkness comes the cry,
The cry that all is lost;
Then e'en Cortes takes up the shout,
And o'er the host 'tis tossed.

Some place their safety in the stream,
But sink beneath the tide,
E'en others crossing on the dead,
Thus reach the other side.

Surrounded and alone he sits,
Upon his faithful steed;
Here Alvarado clears a space,
But none might share the deed –

For darkness of that murky night
Hides deeds of brightest fame,
Which in the ages yet to come,
Would light the hero's name.

His faithful charger now hath fallen,
Pierced to the very heart.
Quick steps he back, his war cry shouts,
Then onward doth he dart.

Runs he, and leaping high in air,
Fixed does he seem a space,
One instant and the deed is done,
He standeth face to face –

With those who on the other side
Their safety now have found.
The thirst for vengeance satisfied,
The Aztec wheels around.

So, as the sun climbs up the sky,
And shoots his dawning rays,
The foe, as parted by his dart,
Each go their separate ways.

Upon the ground the dead men lie,
Trampled midst gold and gore,
The Aztec toward his temple goes,
For now the fight is o'er.

Follow we not the Spaniard more,
Wending o'er hill and plain,
Suffice to say he reached the coast,
Lost Fortune to regain.

The flame shines brightest e'er goes out,
Thus with the Aztec throne,
On that dark night before the end,
So o'er the fight it shone.

The Montezumas are no more,
Gone is their regal throne,
And freemen live, and rule, and die,
Where they have ruled alone.

Aged 16

Wallace Stevens
1879-1955

'Autumn', which is thought to be Wallace Stevens' first published poem, appeared in his high school magazine in Reading, Pennsylvania during his freshman year at Harvard. Holly Stevens, his daughter and editor, writes: 'The author is given only as "W.S., '97," but no one else in the class had those initials.'

AUTUMN

Long lines of coral light
    And evening star,
One shade that leads the night
    On from afar.

And I keep, sorrowing,
    This sunless zone,
Waiting and resting here,
    In calm alone.

Aged 18

James Joyce
1882-1941

When the first page proofs of his small volume of poems, *Chamber Music*, arrived, James Joyce wrote in some excitement to his brother: 'It is a slim book and on the frontispiece is an open pianner!' He expressed misgivings as well: 'I don't like the book...it is a young man's book. I felt like that. It is not a book of love-verses at all, I perceive. But some of them are pretty enough to be put to music.'

This poem, the second in the book, is said by Stanislaus Joyce to be the earliest of the *Chamber Music* pieces, originally part of an earlier collection and entitled 'Commonplace'.

The twilight turns from amethyst
    To deep and deeper blue,
The lamp fills with a pale green glow
    The trees of the avenue.

The old piano plays an air,
    Sedate and slow and gay;
She bends upon the yellow keys,
    Her head inclines this way.

Shy thoughts and grave wide eyes and hands
    That wander as they list –
The twilight turns to darker blue
    With lights of amethyst.

Aged 18-20

William Carlos Williams
1883-1963

In his autobiography, Williams writes:

> Up to eighteen or even later I had not the slightest intention of writing or doing anything in the arts. Mother painted a little, and both Ed and I consequently painted, using her old tubes and palette which we found in the attic. I know there are several oils still lying around which I perpetrated in those days.
>
> My first poem was born like a bolt out of the blue. It came unsolicited and broke a spell of disillusion and suicidal despondence. Here it is:

> A black, black cloud
> flew over the sun
> driven by fierce flying
> rain.

> The joy I felt, the mysterious, soul-satisfying joy that swept over me at that moment was only mitigated by the critical comment which immediately followed it: How could the clouds be driven by the rain? Stupid.
>
> But joy remained. From that moment I was a poet.

Ezra Pound
1885-1972

At thirteen, Ezra Pound celebrated the end of a school term in verse:

> Four more days until vacation
> Then we leave this —— plantation,
> No more Latin, no more Greek
> No more smoking on the sneak....

Two years later, he decided to be a poet and set himself to learn the necessary skills. He believed that the 'Impulse', as he called it, came from the gods, but that technique was a poet's own responsibility; and so resolved that at thirty he would know more about poetry than any man living.

SONG

> Love thou thy dream
> All base love scorning,
> Love thou the wind
> And here take warning
> That dreams alone can truly be,
> For 'tis in dream I come to thee.

Aged 19

Siegfried Sassoon
1886-1967

This poem, occasioned by a proposal that the length of cricket stumps should be increased, was the first to be published by the poet who in a later poem, 'Dreamers', was to write of soldiers on the Western Front:

> I see them in foul dug-outs, gnawed by rats,
> And in the ruined trenches, lashed by rain,
> Dreaming of things they did with balls and bats...

THE EXTRA INCH

O batsman, rise and go and stop the rot,
And go and stop the rot.
(It was indeed a rot,
Six down for twenty-three).
The batsman thought how wretched was his lot,
And all alone went he.

The bowler bared his mighty, cunning arm,
His vengeance-wreaking arm,
His large yet wily arm,
With fearful powers endowed.
The batsman took his guard. (A deadly calm
Had fallen on the crowd).

O is it a half-volley or long-hop,
A seventh-bounce long-hop,
A fast and fierce long-hop,
That the bowler letteth fly?
The ball was straight and bowled him neck and crop.
He knew not how or why.

Full sad and slow pavilionwards he walked.
The careless critics talked;
Some said that he was yorked;
A half-volley at a pinch.
The batsman murmured as he inward stalked,
'It was the extra inch.'

Aged 16

T.S. Eliot
1888-1965

Eliot told his wife that, at the age of nine or ten, he wrote 'a few little verses about the sadness of having to start school again every Monday morning'. He gave them to his Mother and hoped they had not been preserved. At about fourteen he wrote 'some very gloomy quatrains in the form of the *Rubáiyát'* which had "captured my imagination".' These he showed to no one and presumed destroyed.

He said of 'A Lyric', stanzas in imitation of Ben Jonson: 'My English master, who had set his class the task of producing some verse, was much impressed and asked whether I had had any help from some elder person. Surprised, I assured him that they were wholly unaided'. They were printed in the school paper, *Smith Academy Record*, but he did not mention them to his family. 'Some time later the issue was shown to my Mother, and she remarked (we were walking along Beaumont Street in St Louis) that she thought them better than anything in verse she had ever written. I knew what her verse meant to her. We did not discuss the matter further'.

[A LYRIC]

If Time and Space, as Sages say,
  Are things which cannot be,
The sun which does not feel decay
  No greater is than we.
So why, Love, should we ever pray
  To live a century?
The butterfly that lives a day
  Has lived eternity.

The flowers I gave thee when the dew
  Was trembling on the vine,
Were withered ere the wild bee flew
  To suck the eglantine.
So let us haste to pluck anew
  Nor mourn to see them pine,
And though our days of love be few
  Yet let them be divine.

Aged 16

Isaac Rosenberg
1890-1918

Rosenberg's earliest-known poem, his 'Ode to David's Harp', owes something to Byron's lines beginning 'The harp the monarch minstrel swept'. It can be read as an oblique invocation to the Jewish heritage that would prove his own source of inspiration.

ODE TO DAVID'S HARP

Awake! ye joyful strains, awake!
In silence sleep no more;
Disperse the gloom that ever lies
O'er Judah's barren shore.
Where are the hands that strung thee
With tender touch and true?
Those hands are silenced too.

The harp that faster caused to beat
The heart that throbbed for war,
The harp that melancholy calmed,
Lies mute on Judah's shore.
One chord awake – one strain prolong
To wake the zeal in Israel's breast;
Oh sacred lyre, once more, how long?
'Tis vain, alas! in silence rest.

Many a minstrel fame's elated
Envies thee thy harp of fame,
Harp of David – monarch minstrel,
Bravely – bravely, keep thy name.
Ay! every ear that listen'd,
Was charmed – was thrilled – was bound.
Every eye with moisture glisten'd
Thrilling to the harp's sweet sound.

Hark! the harp is pouring
Notes of burning fire,
And each soul o'erpowering,
Melts the rousing ire.
Fiercer – shriller – wilder far
Than the iron notes of war,
Accents sweet and echoes sweeter,

Minstrel – minstrel, steeds fly fleeter
Spurred on by thy magic strains.

Tell me not the harp lies sleeping,
Set not thus my heart aweeping,
In the muse's fairy dwelling
There thy magic notes are swelling.
But for list'ning mortals' ear
Vainly wait, ye will not hear.
So clearly sweet – so plaintive sad
More tender tone no harper had.
O! when again shall Israel see
A harp so toned with melody?

Aged 15

Edna St. Vincent Millay
1892-1950

In the Foreword to her *Collected Sonnets* – well over 150 of them – Millay reminisced about her first such effort, composed when she was fifteen:

> Some time ago, while looking through the pages of an old work-book, I came upon one poem which I remembered vividly: the first sonnet I ever wrote. This, although it was written as a practice-piece, an exercise in sonnet-composition, and not intended ever to be published, I am printing in this foreword, as an object of possible curiosity and interest to readers of my *Collected Sonnets*.
>
> I was about fifteen, I think, when I wrote it, – not very young to be trying my hand at my first sonnet. (Somewhat young, perhaps, to be burning in my lonely grate packets of letters yellow with age!)
>
> The word 'indisputable', as used in line four, ... is not, I fear, an elegant attempt to stress my syllables after the manner of Shelley, but, rather, a sturdy, whole-hearted mispronunciation.
>
> The word 'cog' at the end of line seven is not brought in just for the rhyme. This is the only part of my first sonnet which may be said to be 'real', as distinct from 'fanciful'. That year for the first time, during the months of my summer-vacation from High School (where I had taken a course in typewriting and stenography) I had a job: I was a typist in a lawyer's office in Camden, Maine.
>
> The phrase 'let slack or swell', in the next to the last line, is not so strained and far-fetched a metaphor as it sounds: it refers to the gradual ebbing and the gradual flooding of the tide, – an expression natural enough to a girl who had lived all her life at the very tide-line of the sea.

OLD LETTERS

I know not why I am so loath to lay
Your yellowed leaves along the glowing log,
Unburied dead, that cling about and clog –
With indisputable, insistent say
Of the stout past's all inefficient fray –
The striving present, rising like a fog
To rust the active me, that am a cog
In the great wheel of industry today.
Yet, somehow, in this visible farewell
To the crude symbols of a simpler creed,
I find a pain that had not parallel
When passed the faith itself, – we give small heed

To incorporeal truth, let slack or swell;
But truth made tangible, is truth indeed.

Aged 15

Wilfred Owen
1893-1918

As a boy, Owen was fascinated by the life and poetry of Keats and, in April 1911, made the first of several pilgrimages to places associated with his favourite poet. He took the train from Torquay to Newton Abbot and along the widening estuary to Teignmouth. There, head down and collar up against 'soft buffeting sheets and misty drifts of Devonshire rain', he went in search of the house where Keats had lived from March to May 1818. He found it and gaped at its bow windows regardless of the people inside, 'who finally became quite alarmed'. Returning, he wrote this poem:

SONNET

WRITTEN AT TEIGNMOUTH, ON A PILGRIMAGE TO KEATS'S HOUSE

Three colours have I known the Deep to wear;
'Tis well today that Purple grandeurs gloom,
Veiling the Emerald sheen and Sky-blue glare.
Well, too, that lowly-brooding clouds now loom
In sable majesty around, fringed fair
With ermine-white of surf: To me they bear
Watery memorials of His mystic doom
Whose Name was writ in Water (saith his tomb).

Eternally may sad waves wail his death,
Choke in their grief 'mongst rocks where he has lain,
Or heave in silence, yearning with hushed breath,
While mournfully trail the slow-moved mists and rain,
And softly the small drops slide from weeping trees,
Quivering in anguish to the sobbing breeze.

Aged 18

E.E. Cummings
1894-1962

In the second of his autobiographical 'non lectures', Edward Estlin Cummings recalled his early encounter with the well-known Harvard philosopher, Josiah Royce:

> One memorable day, our ex-substantialist (deep in structural meditation) met head-on professor Royce; who was rolling peacefully home from a lecture. 'Estlin' his courteous and gentle voice hazarded 'I understand that you write poetry.' I blushed. 'Are you perhaps' he inquired, regarding a particular leaf of a particular tree 'acquainted with the sonnets of Dante Gabriel Rossetti?' I blushed a different blush and shook an ignorant head. 'Have you a moment?' he shyly suggested, less than half looking at me; and just perceptible appended 'I rather imagine you might enjoy them.' Shortly thereafter, sage and ignoramus were sitting opposite each other in a diminutive study (marvellously smelling of tobacco and cluttered with student notebooks of a menacing bluish shade) – the ignoramus listening, enthralled; the sage intoning, lovingly and beautifully, his favourite poems. And very possibly (although I don't, as usual, know) that is the reason – or more likely the unreason – I've been writing sonnets ever since.

'Vision', almost but not quite a sonnet, was the first of Cummings's poems to be published in the *Harvard Monthly*.

VISION

The dim deep of a yellow evening slides
Across the green, and mingles with the elms.
A faint beam totters feebly in the west,
Trembles, and all the earth is wild with light,
Stumbles, and all the world is in the dark.

The huge black sleeps above; – lo, two white stars.

Harvard, your shadow-walls, and ghost-toned tower,
Dim, ancient-moulded, vague, and faint, and far,
Is gone! And through the flesh I see the soul:
Coloring iron in red leaping flame,
The thunder-strokes of mighty, sweating men,
Furious hammers of clashing fierce and high, –
And in a corner of the smithy coiled,
Black, brutal, massive-linked, the toil-wrought chain
Which is to bind God's right hand to the world.

Aged 17

Charles Hamilton Sorley
1895-1915

As a schoolboy at Marlborough College, Sorley's reading of Julius Caesar's *History of the Gallic War* helped him to imagine the construction of Roman fortifications on the crest of the Marlborough Downs. Two years after writing this strangely prophetic poem, he was killed on the Western Front in the First World War.

BARBURY CAMP

We burrowed night and day with tools of lead,
Heaped the bank up and cast it in a ring
And hurled the earth above. And Caesar said,
'Why, it is excellent. I like the thing.'
We, who are dead,
Made it, and wrought, and Caesar liked the thing.

And here we strove, and here we felt each vein
Ice-bound, each limb fast-frozen, all night long.
And here we held communion with the rain
That lashed us into manhood with its thong,
Cleansing through pain.
And the wind visited us and made us strong.

Up from around us, numbers without name,
Strong men and naked, vast, on either hand
Pressing us in, they came. And the wind came
And bitter rain, turning grey all the land.
That was our game,
To fight with men and storms, and it was grand.

For many days we fought them, and our sweat
Watered the grass, making it spring up green,
Blooming for us. And, if the wind was wet,
Our blood wetted the wind, making it keen
With the hatred
And wrath and courage that our blood had been.

So, fighting men and winds and tempests, hot
With joy and hate and battle-lust, we fell
Where we fought. And God said, 'Killed at last then? What!
Ye that are too strong for heaven, too clean for hell,

92

(God said) stir not.
This be your heaven, or, if ye will, your hell.'

So again we fight and wrestle, and again
Hurl the earth up and cast it in a ring.
But when the wind comes up, driving the rain
(Each rain-drop a fiery steed), and the mists rolling
Up from the plain,
This wild procession, this impetuous thing,

Hold us amazed. We mount the wind-cars, then
Whip up the steeds and drive through all the world,
Searching to find somewhere some brethren,
Sons of the winds and waters of the world.
We, who were men,
Have sought, and found no men in all this world.

Wind, that has blown here always ceaselessly,
Bringing, if any man can understand,
Might to the mighty, freedom to the free;
Wind, that has caught us, cleansed us, made us grand,
Wind that is we
(We that were men) – make men in all this land,

That so may live and wrestle and hate that when
They fall at last exultant, as we fell,
And come to God, God may say, 'Do you come then
Mildly enquiring, is it heaven or hell?
Why! Ye were men!
Back to your winds and rains. Be these your heaven and hell!'

Aged 17

Robert Graves
1895-1986

Thirty years after writing his first poem, Graves said: 'The temptation to digress has always vexed me. Indeed, it was the subject of my first poem.... This was about the mocking interruptions of a poet's privacy by a star....'

I sat in my chamber yesternight,
  I lit the lamp, I drew the blind
And I took my pen in hand to write;
  But boisterous winds had rent the blind
  And you were peering from behind –
Peeping Tom in the skies afar,
Bold, inquisitive, impudent star!

Aged 13

Stephen Vincent Benét
1898-1943

'The Hemp' was published in the Christmas issue of *Century* magazine during Benét's first year at Yale University. It had been accepted for publication the preceding summer. Although he had failed thirteen of his Yale entrance examinations, and was hard at work with a tutor, Benét was later to recollect the summer of 1915 fondly:

> But it was a good summer. There was the bright heat of July and August in the air, and the red dust on the clay tennis-court, and the thunderstorm that came every evening to cool things off. There was Boyle's Law and the date of the Reform Bill and the ablative absolute and writing till my feet felt cold. There was my brother's letter saying that the *Century* had accepted 'The Hemp' and John Wolcott Adams was to illustrate it and my father's voice saying the song in 'Lucullus Dines –' was really rather pretty but the blank verse showed the influence of Browning. It was a good time, it was also a culmination, though I did not know that. I was not to come back to Georgia again, except for vacations. And, after that, I began to be someone else.

THE HEMP

I. THE PLANTING OF THE HEMP

Captain Hawk scourged clean the seas
(Black is the gap below the plank)
From the Great North Bank to the Caribbees.
(Down by the marsh the hemp grows rank).

His fear was on the seaport towns,
The weight of his hand held hard the downs.

And the merchants cursed him, bitter and black,
For a red flame in the sea-fog's wrack
Was all of their ships that might come back.

For all he had one word alone,
One clod of dirt in their faces thrown,
'The hemp that shall hang me is not grown!'

His name bestrode the seas like Death,
The waters trembled at his breath.

95

This is the tale of how he fell,
Of the long sweep and the heavy swell,
And the rope that dragged him down to hell.

The fight was done, and the gutted ship,
Stripped like a shark the sea-gulls strip,

Lurched blindly, eaten out with flame,
Back to the land from whence she came,
A skimming horror, an eyeless shame.

And Hawk stood on his quarter-deck,
And saw the sky and saw the wreck.

Below, a butt for sailors' jeers,
White as the sky when a white squall nears,
Huddled the crowd of the prisoners.

Over the bridge of the tottering plank,
Where the sea shook and the gulf yawned blank,
They shrieked and struggled and dropped and sank.

Pinioned arms and hands bound fast.
One girl alone was left at last.

Sir Henry Gaunt was a mighty lord.
He sat in state at the Council board.

The governors were as naught to him.
From one rim to the other rim
Of his great plantations, flung out wide
Like a purple cloak, was a full month's ride.

Life and death in his white hands lay,
And his only daughter stood at bay,
Trapped like a hare in the toils that day.

He sat at wine in his gold and his lace,
And far away, in a bloody place,
Hawk came near, and she covered her face.

He rode in the fields, and the hunt was brave,
And far away, his daughter gave

A shriek that the seas cried out to hear,
And he could not see and he could not save.

Her white soul withered in the mire
As paper shrivels up in fire,
And Hawk laughed, and he kissed her mouth,
And her body he took for his desire.

II. THE GROWING OF THE HEMP

Sir Henry stood in the manor room,
And his eyes were hard gems in the gloom.

And he said, 'Go, dig me furrows five
Where the green marsh creeps like a thing alive –
There at its edge where the rushes thrive.'

And where the furrows rent the ground
He sowed the seed of hemp around.

And the blacks shrink back and are sore afraid
At the furrows five that rib the glade,
And the voodoo work of the master's spade.

For a cold wind blows from the marshland near,
And white things move, and the night grows drear,
And they chatter and crouch and are sick with fear.

But down by the marsh, where the grey slaves glean,
The hemp sprouts up, and the earth is seen
Veiled with a tenuous mist of green.

And Hawk still scourges the Caribbees,
And many men kneel at his knees.

Sir Henry sits in his house alone,
And his eyes are hard and dull like stone.

And the waves beat, and the winds roar,
And all things are as they were before.

And the days pass, and the weeks pass,
And nothing changes but the grass.

But down where the fireflies are like eyes,
And the damps shudder, and the mists rise,
The hemp-stalks stand up toward the skies.

And down from the poop of the pirate ship
A body falls, and the great sharks grip.

Innocent, lovely, go in grace!
At last there is peace upon your face.

And Hawk laughs loud as the corpse is thrown,
'The hemp that shall hang me is not grown!'

Sir Henry's face is iron to mark,
And he gazes ever in the dark.

And the days pass, and the weeks pass,
And the world is as it always was.

But down by the marsh the sickles beam,
Glitter on glitter, gleam on gleam,
And the hemp falls down by the stagnant stream.

And Hawk beats up from the Caribbees,
Swooping to pounce in the Northern seas.

Sir Henry sits sunk deep in his chair,
And white as his hand is grown his hair.

And the days pass, and the weeks pass,
And the sands roll from the hourglass.

But down by the marsh, in the blazing sun,
The hemp is smoothed and twisted and spun.
The rope made, and the work done.

III. THE USING OF THE HEMP

Captain Hawk scourged clean the seas,
(Black is the gap below the plank)
From the Great North Bank to the Caribbees
(Down by the marsh the hemp grows rank)

He sailed in the broad Atlantic track
And the ships that saw him came not back.

Till once again, where the wide tides ran,
He stopped to harry a merchantman.

He bade her stop. Ten guns spoke true
From her hidden ports, and a hidden crew,
Hacking his great ship, through and through.

Dazed and dumb with the sudden death,
He scarce had time to draw a breath

Before the grappling-irons bit deep
And the boarders slew his crew like sheep.

Hawk stood up straight, his breast to the steel;
His cutlass made a bloody wheel.

His cutlass made a wheel of flame.
They shrank before him as he came.

And the bodies fell in a choking crowd,
And still he thundered out aloud,

'The hemp that shall hang me is not grown!'
They fled at last. He was left alone.

Before his foe Sir Henry stood.
'The hemp is grown and my word made good!'

And the cutlass clanged with a hissing whir
On the lashing blade of the rapier.

Hawk roared and charged like a maddened buck.
As the cobra strikes, Sir Henry struck,

Pouring his life in a single thrust,
And the cutlass shivered to sparks and dust.

Sir Henry stood on the blood-stained deck,
And set his foot on his foe's neck.

Then, from the hatch, where the torn decks slope,
Where the dead roll and the wounded grope,
He dragged the serpent of the rope.

The sky was blue and the sea was still,
The waves lapped softly, hill on hill,
And between one wave and another wave
The doomed man's cries were little and shrill.

The sea was blue and the sky was calm,
The air dripped with a golden balm.
Like a wind-blown fruit between sea and sun,
A black thing writhed at a yard-arm.

Slowly then, and awesomely,
The ship sank, and the gallows-tree,
And there was nought between sea and sun –
Nought but the sun and the sky and the sea.

But down by the marsh, where the fever breeds,
Only the water chuckles and pleads;
For the hemp clings fast to a dead man's throat,
And blind Fate gathers back her seeds.

Aged 17

Sir John Betjeman
1906-1984

Bells sound repeatedly through Betjeman's poetry from his schoolboy
stanzas to the celebrated autobiographical work *Summoned by Bells*,
(1960). The 'poet's rhymes' referred to in 'Dawn' may be 'The Bells' by
Edgar Allan Poe.

DAWN

Ever ting-a-linging my bedroom clock is ringing,
    Ringing, ringing,
As the sun breaks in the east;
      And, stretching with a yawn,
      I curse the lovely dawn,
And wait in moody silence till the bedroom clock has ceased.

I've read the poet's rhymes about early morning chimes
    At awful times;
And the sun through window panes;
      The little birds twitting
      And the big ones flitting.
But poets *never* write about the dawning when it rains.

Aged 13

Louis MacNeice
1907-1963

In his book *Modern Poetry: A Personal Essay*, MacNeice recalled that from the age of seven

> I wrote poems myself. What I was chiefly interested in was the pattern of the words. My recipe for a poem was simple – use 'thou' instead of 'you' and make the ends of the lines rhyme with each other; no specific emotion or 'poetic' content required. Here is a poem about a live parrot which I had seen in a neighbour's house:

> O parrot, thou hast grey feathers
> which thou peckest in all weathers
> And thy curled beak
> Could make me squeak;
> Thy tail I admire
> As red as the fire
> And as red as a carrot,
> Thy tail I admire,
> Thou cross old parrot.

> This seems to me now to be better than much which I afterwards wrote in the fervour of my adolescence. There is a nucleus of observed fact, and my naïve idea that putting anything into rhyme makes it a poem at least enabled me to convey this fact in memorable form (I use the word memorable in its literal sense, which is its basic sense, because I find this poem easy to remember).

When, as a schoolboy at Marlborough, he first published a poem in the school magazine, it showed him to be steeped in the early poetry of his fellow-countryman, W.B. Yeats.

DEATH OF A PROMINENT BUSINESS MAN

'Who are you that are twisted, brown,
Come to knock at the window pane?
I have got to attend to my business cares,
My speculations, my stocks and shares,
So leave me alone again.'
'One of the wee folk out of the hills
I clammer and hammer your window pane;
For your stocks and shares may wither and rot
E'er God forgets the forget-me-not;
And I NEVER will leave you alone again.
Come you away to the black peat bog,
The driving sleet and the drifting rain,

Where the wee folk weave from the pith of the reed
And the world is rid of financial greed
And the gentry dance in a chain.'
The shriek of an owl and the flit of a bat
And a single drop of rain,
And the old man's body lay dead in his chair,
But his soul had gone to taste the air
Away on the hills again.

Aged 17

W.H. Auden
1907-1973

Wystan Hugh Auden began writing poetry at the age of fifteen, because, as he tells us, 'one Sunday afternoon in March 1922, a friend suggested that I should: the thought had never occurred to me.' The following year he discovered Walter de la Mare's anthology *Come Hither*, which introduced him to a range of new models, among them Robert Frost and Thomas Hardy. Hardy's impact was immediate: 'For more than a year I read no one else. I smuggled [his books] into class, carried them about on Sunday walks, and took them up to the dormitory to read in the early morning, though they were far too unwieldy to read in bed with comfort.' 'The Traction Engine', which Auden never published, was written in this period of Hardyesque experimentation.

THE TRACTION ENGINE

Its days are over now; no farmyard airs
Will quiver hot above its chimney-stack; the fairs
It dragged from green to green are not what they have been
        In previous years.

Here now it lies, unsheltered, undesired,
Its engine rusted fast, its boiler mossed, unfired,
Companioned by a boot-heel and an old cart-wheel,
        In thistles attired,

Unfeeling, uncaring; imaginings
Mar not the future; no past sick memory clings,
Yet it seems well to deserve the love we reserve
        For animate things.

Aged 16/17

Stephen Spender
b. 1909

In his autobiography, *World within World*, Spender writes of his Aunt
May:

Sometimes she talked to me about the East (which she called *her*
East) for which she had a Great Passion. She was excellent at Early
Morning Bedroom Scenes, when she would summon me to her room
and, after explaining that she was in bed because the snares which
surrounded me had kept her awake all night, she would tell me her
Night Thoughts, full of forebodings on my account. After one of these
occasions, I wrote at the age of seventeen a poem opening with lines
which capture, I think, a little of my aunt's vigour:

Madam, your face half-hidden by your hair
Which hung in tousled patterns from the fair
Massively active flesh, surrounded by great pillows,
You were the largest of your bed's huge billows!
Reclining there, incarnate confidence,
You chid me for my lack of competence
In the half-curtained room. Warm shadows fell
Round you, like guardian ghosts. I did not tell
You of them, being sure that you
Would think this an aesthetic thing to do.
And most aesthetic was the mad March wind
Which rashly rapped against the window blind....

Dylan Thomas
1914-1953

Thomas entered Swansea Grammar School, where his father was senior English master, shortly before his eleventh birthday. His stay was not conspicuously successful; although his father had hoped he would attend university, Dylan eventually failed his examinations in all subjects except English. Years later, in his radio play *Return Journey*, he recreated his schoolmaster's impressions in free verse:

> Oh yes, I remember him well, the boy you are searching for:
> he looked like most boys, no better, brighter or more respectful
> he cribbed, mitched, spilt ink, rattled his desk and
> garbled his lessons with the worst of them...

He was 'thirty-third in trigonometry', the Schoolmaster concludes, 'and, as might be expected, edited the School Magazine.' The following Song appeared in it his first term.

THE SONG OF THE MISCHIEVOUS DOG

> There are many who say that a dog has his day,
> And a cat has a number of lives;
> There are others who think that a lobster is pink,
> And that bees never work in their hives.
> There are fewer, of course, who insist that a horse
> Has a horn and two humps on its head,
> And a fellow who jests that a mare can build nests
> Is as rare as a donkey that's red.
> Yet in spite of all this, I have moments of bliss,
> For I cherish a passion for bones,
> And though doubtful of biscuit, I'm willing to risk it,
> And love to chase rabbits and stones.
> But my greatest delight is to take a good bite
> At a calf that is plump and delicious;
> And if I indulge in a bite at a bulge,
> Let's hope you won't think me too vicious.

Aged 11

David Gascoyne
b. 1916

Music made a greater initial impact than literature on the young David Gascoyne. The first poem he remembers being taught was de la Mare's 'Silver', and in 1929 the magazine of the Salisbury Cathedral Choristers' School printed a page of 'Four of Several Poems written by D.G. (Chorister)', the last of which, composed when he was twelve, ended:

> 'The lawns of the Close, dim white outspread,
> Are like that on the sea', I said.
> 'This Autumn is but a stage,
> A step, on the house of my pilgrimage.'

At fourteen, Gascoyne moved to London and the Regent Street Polytechnic Secondary School, where he became increasingly aware of what was going on in contemporary poetry. He writes:

> There is little trace of immediate topicality in my first published poem, a 28-line effort entitled 'Transformation Scene', which appeared in the weekly magazine *Everyman* before I left, or rather was asked to leave, school, having proved hopeless exam-fodder. It was reprinted in the collection *Roman Balcony*, also published in 1932 while I was still going to school. The main influence to be detected in this precocious collection of juvenilia is that of the Imagists, whom I had read for a while extensively. The title almost certainly echoes a then recent reading of Pater's *Marius the Epicurean*, and reflects a concern with 'the Decline of the West', a constant implicit theme in nearly all my poetry to date, the Roman Empire's decline and fall representing an immature metaphor for the continually increasing social and spiritual crisis experienced by my generation and its successors.

MOOD

The trees are dead.
There are no wood-nymphs here;
But among the grey branches
Delicately interlaced with lichens
A diabolic countenance may peer.

No brilliant bird
Will call from the sapless bough.
An ashen silence overpowers the wood.
The fauns are fled for brighter lawns.
Strange are the solitudes that fade here now,

Far off, perhaps,
A shadowy lake among bleak hills decays:
But here there are no waters but the pools
That stagnant lie among brown leaves,
The condensation of dead days.

Aged 16

Keith Douglas
1920-1944

The son of a soldier, Keith Douglas was from earliest childhood attracted by the glamour of soldiering. At the age of ten he wrote a poem called 'Waterloo', which began:

> Napoleon is charging our squares,
> with his cavalry he is attacking;
> let the enemy do what he dares,
> our soldiers in braveness aren't lacking.

Fourteen years later, a veteran of the North African campaign, he was killed in the Allied invasion of Normandy.

.303

I have looked through the pine-trees
Cooling their sun-warmed needles in the night,
I saw the moon's face white
　　Beautiful as the breeze.

Yet you have seen the boughs sway with the night's breath,
Wave like dead arms, repudiating the stars
And the moon, circular and useless, pass
　　Pock-marked with death.

Through a machine-gun's sights
I saw men curse, weep, cough, sprawl in their entrails;
You did not know the gardener in the vales,
　　Only efficiency delights you.

Aged 15

Sidney Keyes
1922-1943

Sidney Keyes lived with his paternal grandfather, after whom he was named, until the age of ten. He was in his third year of school at Tonbridge when his grandfather died in April 1938; the following spring he wrote a moving elegy for the first anniversary of his grandfather's death.

ELEGY
(In memoriam S.K.K.)

April again, and it is a year again
Since you walked out and slammed the door
Leaving us tangled in your words. Your brain
Lives in the bank-book, and your eyes look up
Laughing from the carpet on the floor:
And we still drink from your silver cup.

It is a year again since they poured
The dumb ground into your mouth:
And yet we know, by some recurring word
Or look caught unawares, that you still drive
Our thoughts like the smart cobs of your youth –
When you and the world were alive.

A year again, and we have fallen on bad times
Since they gave you to the worms.
I am ashamed to take delight in these rhymes
Without grief; but you need no tears.
We shall never forget nor escape you, nor make terms
With your enemies, the swift departing years.

Aged 16

Philip Larkin
1922-1985

Larkin wrote ceaselessly in his schooldays: 'now verse, which I sewed up into little books, now prose, a thousand words a night after homework.' His poem 'Ultimatum', the first to be published in a national magazine (*The Listener* for 28 November 1940), is the work of someone for whom, as he said, 'Auden was the only alternative to "old-fashioned" poetry'. It explores a theme to which he would return in such of his later poems as 'Poetry of Departures', which ends:

> But I'd go today,
>
> Yes, swagger the nut-strewn roads,
> Crouch in the fo'c'sle
> Stubbly with goodness, if
> It weren't so artificial,
> Such a deliberate step backwards
> To create an object:
> Books; china; a life
> Reprehensibly perfect.

ULTIMATUM

But we must build our walls, for what we are
Necessitates it, and we must construct
The ship to navigate behind them, there.
Hopeless to ignore, helpless instruct
For any term of time beyond the years
That warn us of the need for emigration:
Exploded the ancient saying: Life is yours.

For on our island is no railway station,
There are no tickets for the Vale of Peace,
No docks where trading ships and seagulls pass.

Remember stories you read when a boy
– The shipwrecked sailor gaining safety by
His knife, tree trunk, and lianas – for now
You must escape, or perish saying no.

Aged 17

James K. Baxter
1926-1972

In his autobiographical lecture, 'Notes on the Education of a New Zealand Poet', Baxter tells us:

> The first poem I wrote was no doubt significant, if not in its form or content, at least in the way I approached the writing of it. I climbed up to a hole in a bank in a hill above the sea, and there fell into the attitude of *listening* out of which poems may rise – not to the sound of the sea, but to the unheard sound of which poems are translations – it was then that I first endured that intense effort of *listening*, like a man chained to the ground trying to stand upright and walk – and from this intensity of *listening* the words emerged –

> O Ocean, in thy rocky bed
> The starry fishes swim about –
> There coral rocks are strewn around
> Like some great temple on the ground...

> I was then seven years old. I don't think my methods of composition have changed much since that time. The daimon has always to be invoked; and there is no certainty that he will answer the invitation.

Baxter's first collection of poems, *Beyond the Palisade*, was published when he was eighteen years old.

THE FIRST FORGOTTEN

O fons Bandusiae
The green hill-orchard where
My great-granduncle lived
Is overgrown: no cache and no reprieve

The chilly air holds: they came from the
Old lands; for hunger; or fearing the young
Would shoot from thicket a keeper
Be transported or hung.

So beholding the strange reeds
Arrogant flax and fen
They saw release, eventual and ancestral peace
Building the stubborn clans again.

Bee-hives along an elderberry fence....
The land is drained: gorse

Only will grow: to the towns now
Their sons' sons gone, expanding universe.

A light and brittle birth.
I would glorify
Innumerable men in whose breasts my heart once beat
Is beating: they were slow to die.

One who drove a bullock-team
In the gold-rush on an upland track.
One smiling and whistling softly
With a horse-shoe behind his back.

Steel mutilates: more the hollow
Facade, the gaudy mask
On a twisted face: clay-shut, forgetful, shall
They answer? we ask?

Only the rough and paper bark peeling
From young blue-gums; while undergrowth
Among stunted apple-trees coiling
Trips the foot: sods grass-buried like antique faith.

Aged 18

Sylvia Plath
1932-1963

Sylvia Plath had her first poem published in the *Boston Sunday Herald* when she was only eight years old, and she remained prolific throughout childhood and adolescence. The vision of the sea in her poem about Ariadne – abandoned by her lover Theseus on the island of Dia (Naxos) – was to recur in her later poetry. 'My childhood landscape,' she wrote in her autobiographical essay 'OCEAN 1212-W', 'was not land but the end of land – the cold, salt, running hills of the Atlantic. I sometimes think my vision of the sea is the clearest thing I own. I pick it up, exile that I am, like the purple "lucky stones" I used to collect with a white ring all the way round, or the shell of a blue mussel with its rainbowy angel's fingernail interior; and in one wash of memory the colours deepen and gleam, the early world draws breath.'

TO ARIADNE
(deserted by Theseus)

Oh, fury, equalled only by the shrieking wind –
The lashing of the waves against the shore,
You rage in vain, waist deep into the sea,
Betrayed, deceived, forsaken ever more.

Your cries are lost, your curses are unheard by him
That treads his winged way above the cloud.
The honeyed words upon your lips are brine;
The bitter salt wind sings off-key and loud.

Oh, scream in vain for vengeance now, and beat your hands
In vain against the dull impassive stone.
The cold waves break and shatter at your feet;
The sky is mean – and you bereft, alone.

The white-hot rage abates, and then – futility.
You lean exhausted on the rock. The sea
Begins to calm, and the retreating storm
But grumbles faintly, while the black clouds flee.

And now the small waves break like green glass, frilled with foam;
The fickle sun sends darts of light to land.
Why do you stand and listen only to
The sobbing of the wind along the sand?

Aged 16

Seamus Heaney
b. 1939

Laurence Lerner, who was a lecturer at Queens University, Belfast, during Heaney's time there as an undergraduate, commended the phrase 'gorse-pricked with gold' when his poem 'October Thought' first appeared in a student magazine. Heaney writes:

> It was published under the pseudonym 'Incertus' and while this earliest brush with a critical audience did not altogether confer the longed-for certitude, it did suggest that words I wrote might sometimes be capable of transmitting a live signal. Yet the words were more Hopkins' than mine; and yet again, while they were overdone and pastiche, they opened a seam of phonetic ore that kept tempting me to come back and try again. This was among the first four or five attempts I made at writing verse and is, I suppose, the 'best' of them.

OCTOBER THOUGHT

Starling thatch watches, and sudden swallow
Straight breaks to its mud-nest, home-rest rafter,
Up through dry, dust-drunk cobwebs like laughter
Flitting the roof of black-oak, bog-sod and rods of willow;
And twittering flirtings in the eaves as sparrows quarrel.
Haystalks, straw-broken and strewn,
Hide, hear mice mealing the grain, gnawing strong
The iron-bound, swollen and ripe-round corn-barrel.

Minute movement millionfold whispers twilight
Under heaven-hue, plum-blue and gorse-pricked with gold,
And under the knuckle-gnarl of branches, poking the night,
Comes the trickling tinkle of bells well in the fold.

Aged 19

Sources and Acknowledgements

The editor and publishers gratefully acknowledge permission to use copyright material in this book as follows:

W.H. Auden: 'The Traction Engine', from ms in the Bodleian Library, Oxford. Copyright © 1987 by the Estate of W.H. Auden. Reprinted by permission of Edward Mendelson, the Literary Executor.

James K. Baxter: 'The First Forgotten' from *Beyond the Palisade* (1944), reprinted in *Collected Poems*. Copyright © 1979 Oxford University Press (New Zealand), reprinted by permission. Headnote from 'Notes on the Education of a New Zealand Poet', *The Man on the Horse* (1967). Copyright © 1987 by Mrs J.C. Baxter, reprinted by permission.

Stephen Vincent Benet: 'The Hemp' from *The Selected Works of Stephen Vincent Benet*. Copyright © 1916, renewed © 1944 by Stephen Vincent Benet. Reprinted by permission of Brandt & Brandt Literary Agents Inc.

John Betjeman: 'Dawn', from *The Draconian*, the Dragon School magazine. Copyright © 1987 The Estate of John Betjeman. Reprinted by permission of John Murray (Publishers) Ltd.

e.e. cummings: 'Vision' from *The Harvard Monthly* (November 1911), vol. LIII, no.2, p.43. Copyright © 1911, 1958 by e.e. cummings. The quotation from *i: six non-lectures* is reprinted by permission of Harvard University Press. Copyright © 1953 by e.e. cummings, © renewed 1981 by E.E. Cummings Trust.

Emily Dickinson: [A Valentine] Reprinted by permission of the Publishers and the Trustees of Amherst College from *The Poems of Emily Dickinson*, edited by Thomas H. Johnson, Cambridge, Mass.: The Belknap Press of Harvard University Press, Copyright 1951, © 1955, 1979, 1983 by the President and Fellows of Harvard College.

Keith Douglas: '.303' from *The Complete Poems of Keith Douglas*, edited by Desmond Graham, 1978. Copyright © Marie J. Douglas 1978. Reprinted by permission of Oxford University Press.

T.S. Eliot: 'A Lyric' from *Poems Written in Early Youth* by T.S. Eliot. Copyright © 1967 by Valerie Eliot. Reprinted by permission of Faber and Faber Ltd, and Farrar, Straus and Giroux Inc.

Robert Frost: 'La Noche Triste' from *Robert Frost: Poetry and Prose*, edited by Edward Connery Latham and Lawrance Thompson. Copyright © 1972 by Holt, Rinehart and Winston. First published in the *High School Bulletin* (Lawrence, Mass.), April 1890, vol. XI, no.8, pp.1-2. Reprinted by permission of Holt, Rinehart and Winston, Publishers.

David Gascoyne: 'Mood' from *Roman Balcony*, Copyright © 1932, 1987 by David Gascoyne. Reprinted by permission of the author.

Robert Graves: [I sat in my chamber] from *Robert Graves: His Life and Work* by Martin Seymour-Smith, Hutchinson, 1983. Reprinted by permission of A.P. Watt Ltd. on behalf of the Executors of the Estate of Robert Graves.

Thomas Hardy: 'Domicilium' from *The Complete Poems of Thomas Hardy*, edited by James Gibson, 1976. Copyright © 1976 by Macmillan London Ltd. Reprinted by permission of Macmillan London Ltd.

Seamus Heaney: 'October Thought', first printed in *Q* (Q.U.B.) 1959. Reprinted by permission of the author. Copyright © 1987 by Seamus Heaney.

James Joyce: Poem II from *Chamber Music*. From *Collected Poems*. Copyright © 1918 by B.W. Huebsch. Copyright 1927, 1936 by James Joyce, © renewed 1946 by Nora Joyce. Reprinted by permission of Viking Penguin Inc; of Jonathan Cape Ltd; and of the Society of Authors as the literary representative of the Estate of James Joyce.

Sidney Keyes: 'Elegy' from *The Collected Poems of Sidney Keyes*, edited by Michael Meyer, 1945. Reprinted by permission of Routledge & Kegan Paul plc.

Philip Larkin: 'Ultimatum', printed in *The Listener*, 28 November 1940. Reprinted by permission of the Literary Executors of the Larkin Estate.

Amy Lowell: 'Chacago' from ms in the Houghton Library, Harvard University. Reprinted by permission of the Houghton Library.

Louis MacNeice: 'Death of a Prominent Businessman' from *The Malburian*, vol. LIX, p.134; extract from *Modern Poetry* (1938). Reprinted by permission of David Higham Associates Ltd.

Edna St Vincent Millay: 'Old Letters' and headnote from 'Foreword', *Collected Sonnets*, 1941. *Collected Poems*, Harper & Row. Copyright © 1941, 1968 by Edna St Vincent Millay and Norma Millay Ellis. Reprinted by permission of Norma Millay Ellis.

Wilfred Owen: 'Sonnet, written at Teignmouth' from *The Complete Poems and Fragments*, edited by Jon Stallworthy, 1983. Copyright © 1983 the Executors of Harold Owen's Estate. Reprinted by permission of Chatto and Windus Ltd and New Directions Publishing Corporation.

Sylvia Plath: 'To Ariadne' from *Letters Home: Correspondence 1950-1963* edited by Aurelia Schober, Harper & Row, New York; Faber and Faber, London. Copyright © 1975 by Ted Hughes. Reprinted by permission of Olwyn Hughes.

Ezra Pound: 'Song' from *Collected Early Poems of Ezra Pound*, edited by Michael John King, 1976. Copyright © 1926, 1935, 1954, 1965, 1971, 1976 by the Trustees of the Ezra Pound Literary Property Trust. Reprinted by permission of Faber and Faber Ltd and New Directions Publishing Corporation.

Isaac Rosenberg: 'Ode to David's Harp' from *The Collected Works of Isaac*

Fyfield *Books*

"The Fyfield Books series provides an admirable service in publishing good inexpensive selections from the works of interesting but neglected poets"

— British Book News

THOMAS LOVELL BEDDOES (1803-49)
Selected Poems
edited by Judith Higgens

THE BRONTË SISTERS
Selected Poems
edited by Stevie Davies

ELIZABETH BARRETT BROWNING (1806-61)
Selected Poems
edited by Malcolm Hicks

THOMAS CAMPION (1567-1620)
Ayres and Observations
edited by Joan Hart

GEORGE CHAPMAN (?1559-1634)
Selected Poems
edited by Eirean Wain

THOMAS CHATTERTON (1752-70)
Selected Poems
edited by Grevel Lindop

CHARLES COTTON (1630-87)
Selected Poems
edited by Ken Robinson

WILLIAM COWPER (1731-1800)
Selected Poems
edited by Nick Rhodes

GEORGE CRABBE (1754-1832)
Selected Poems
edited by Jem Poster

RICHARD CRASHAW (1612/13-49)
Selected Poems
edited by Michael Cayley

MICHAEL DRAYTON (1563-1631)
Selected Poems
edited by Vivian Thomas

GEORGE GASCOIGNE (1530-77)
The Green Knight:
selected poems and prose
edited by Roger Pooley

JOHN GAY (1685-1732)
Selected Poems
edited by Marcus Walsh

JOHN GOWER (1330-1408)
Selected Poetry
edited by Carole Weinberg

THOMAS GRAY (1716-71)
Selected Poems
edited by John Heath-Stubbs

ROBERT HENRYSON (1425?-1508?)
Selected Poems
edited by W.R.J. Barron

ROBERT HERRICK (1591-1674)
Selected Poems
edited by David Jesson-Dibley

THOMAS HOCCLEVE (?1348-1430)
Selected Poems
edited by Bernard O'Donoghue

BEN JONSON (1572-1637)
Epigrams & The Forest
edited by Richard Dutton

WALTER SAVAGE LANDOR (1775-1864)
Selected Poems and Prose
edited by Keith Hanley

ANDREW MARVELL (1621-78)
Selected Poems
edited by Bill Hutchings

GEORGE MEREDITH (1828-1909)
Selected Poems
edited by Keith Hanley

CHARLES OF ORLEANS (1394-1465)
Selected Poems
edited by Sally Purcell

SIR WALTER RALEGH (?1554-1618)
Selected Writings
edited by Gerald Hammond

JOHN WILMOT, EARL OF ROCHESTER
(1648-80)
The Debt to Pleasure
edited by John Adlard

CHRISTINA ROSSETTI (1830-94)
Selected Poems
edited by C.H. Sisson

SIR PHILIP SIDNEY (1554-86)
Selected Poetry and Prose
edited by Richard Dutton

JOHN SKELTON (1460-1529)
Selected Poems
edited by Gerald Hammond

CHRISTOPHER SMART (1722-71)
Selected Poems
edited by Marcus Walsh

DONALD STANFORD (editor)
Three Poets of the Rhymers' Club:
Lionel Johnson, Ernest Dowson,
John Davidson

HENRY HOWARD, EARL OF SURREY
(1517-47)
Selected Poems
edited by Dennis Keene

JONATHAN SWIFT (1667-1745)
Selected Poems
edited by C.H. Sisson

ALGERNON CHARLES SWINBURNE
(1837-1909)
Selected Poems
edited by L.M. Findlay

ARTHUR SYMONS (1865-1945)
Selected Writings
edited by R.V. Holdsworth

THOMAS TRAHERNE (?1637-74)
Selected Writings
edited by Dick Davis

HENRY VAUGHAN (1622-95)
Selected Poems
edited by Robert B. Shaw

ANNE FINCH, COUNTESS OF WINCHILSEA
(1661-1720)
Selected Poems
edited by Denys Thompson

EDWARD YOUNG (1683-1765)
Selected Poems
edited by Brian Hepworth

"Carcanet are doing an excellent job in this series: the editions are labours of love, not just commercial enterprises. I hope they are familiar to all readers and teachers of literature."
— *Times Literary Supplement*